The Seasons of Madeline Island

A Camera's Eye View

Inspired by the Spirit of Madeline Island and

All the Powers that Be

The Photography of Sheelagh Dalziel

The Seasons of Madeline Island
A Camera's Eye View

The Photography of Sheelagh Dalziel

ISBN: 978-0-692-59333-2
Library of Congress Control Number: 2015920740

For information, address
Motherwell Photography
608-422-2746
motherwellphoto@gmail.com

Book Design: Barbara With
Back Photo: Lisa Jacobson, Sheboygan, WI

This book is dedicated to

God the Father, Creator, Great Spirit.

Marina Lachecki - anam kara, sensei, spiritual guide and mentor.

Gwen Smith Patterson - kalayan mita, best friend, fellow photographer,
fellow journeyer on the Path.

Their love and everlasting support and confidence
made this possible.

Thanks to

The Community of Madeline Island and St. John's United Church of Christ for welcome and belonging.

Barbara With, for her cheerful help with navigating the world of publishing and awesome design skills.

Michael and Cynthia Dalzell who brought me to the Island, little knowing the blessing they were bestowing.

What is Motherwell Photography?

What is Motherwell?

Motherwell is a small town in the County of Lanarkshire Scotland, just down the Clyde River from Glasgow. This town and county are the area that my ancestors came from and where my kin still reside. The Clyde is part of the unofficial boarder between lowland Scotland and the Highlands. Having visited both areas I continue to perceive a connection with the highlanders both in their homeland and in the areas they settled in America such as western North Carolina, eastern Tennessee, and the mountains of northern Pennsylvania.

What is Sheelagh (pronounced like "Sheila") Dalziel (pronounced in the Scottish as "D'Yell")?

What I am is a spiritual being who is learning to look at the world with my inner eye. What that eye sees through the lens of my camera is not always what my physical eye is aiming for. Hence the surprises when I see what the camera captures. That part of myself is looking for the different, the story-telling, the startling aspects of the world we walk around in. So a faded rainbow becomes an artistic arc of color and light and dark; a sprig of new growth on an unidentified bush sends a message of joy and praise to the Creator of all nature; and the landing of a flock of geese in the evening dusk is an impressionistic watercolor.

What is Motherwell Photography?

Motherwell Photography is an expression of my spiritual growth in wonder, laughter, song, and Celtic mysticism. There is in me an imperative to share the gifts given with all those around me. I hope this book can be the medium to share these images with the world so others can perceive the Spirit that can be found on Madeline Island.

Sheelagh Dalziel, September 2015

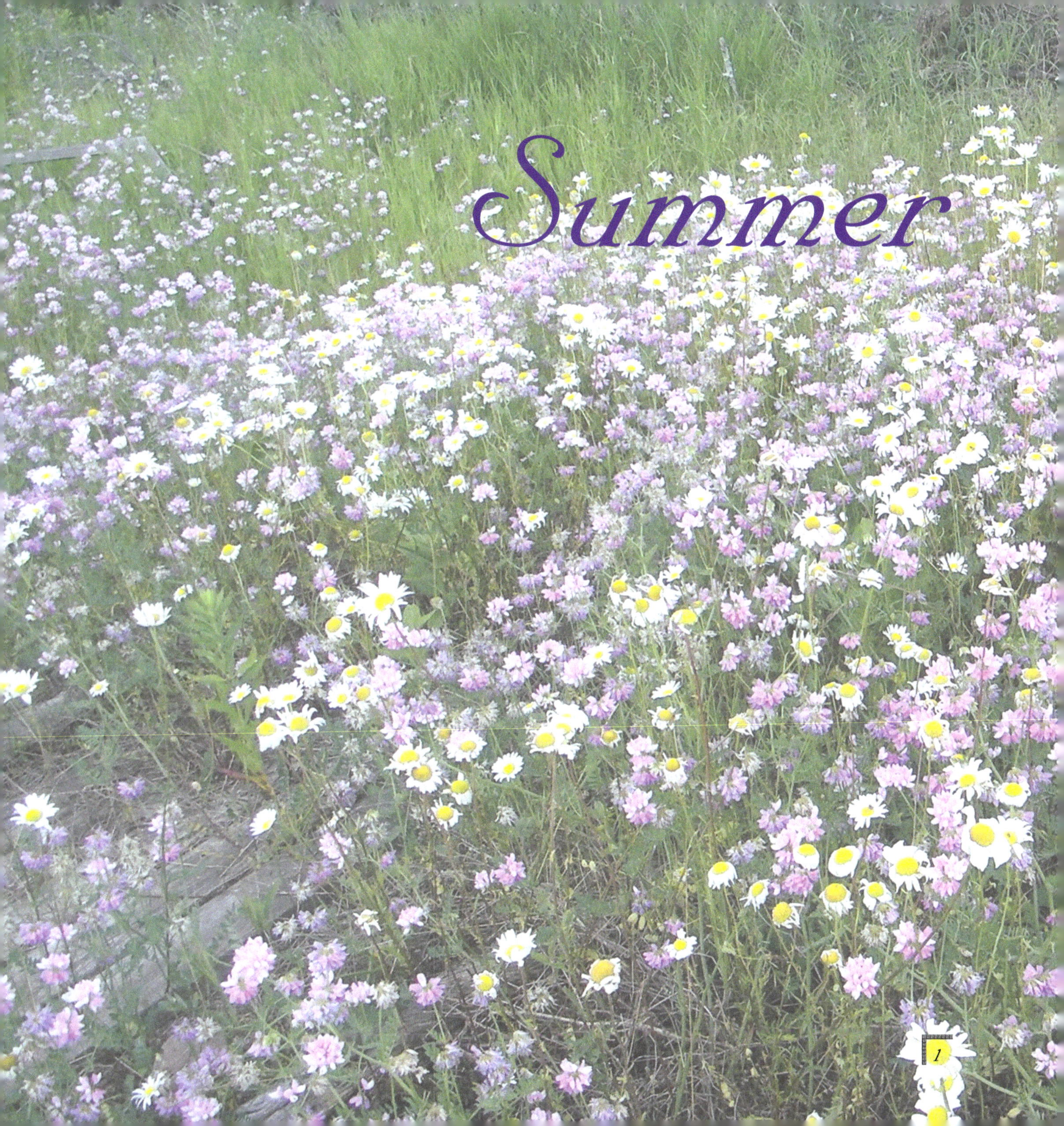
Summer
1

In a May spring riot of blooming daffodils this one,

lone tulip gave promise to June's glory.

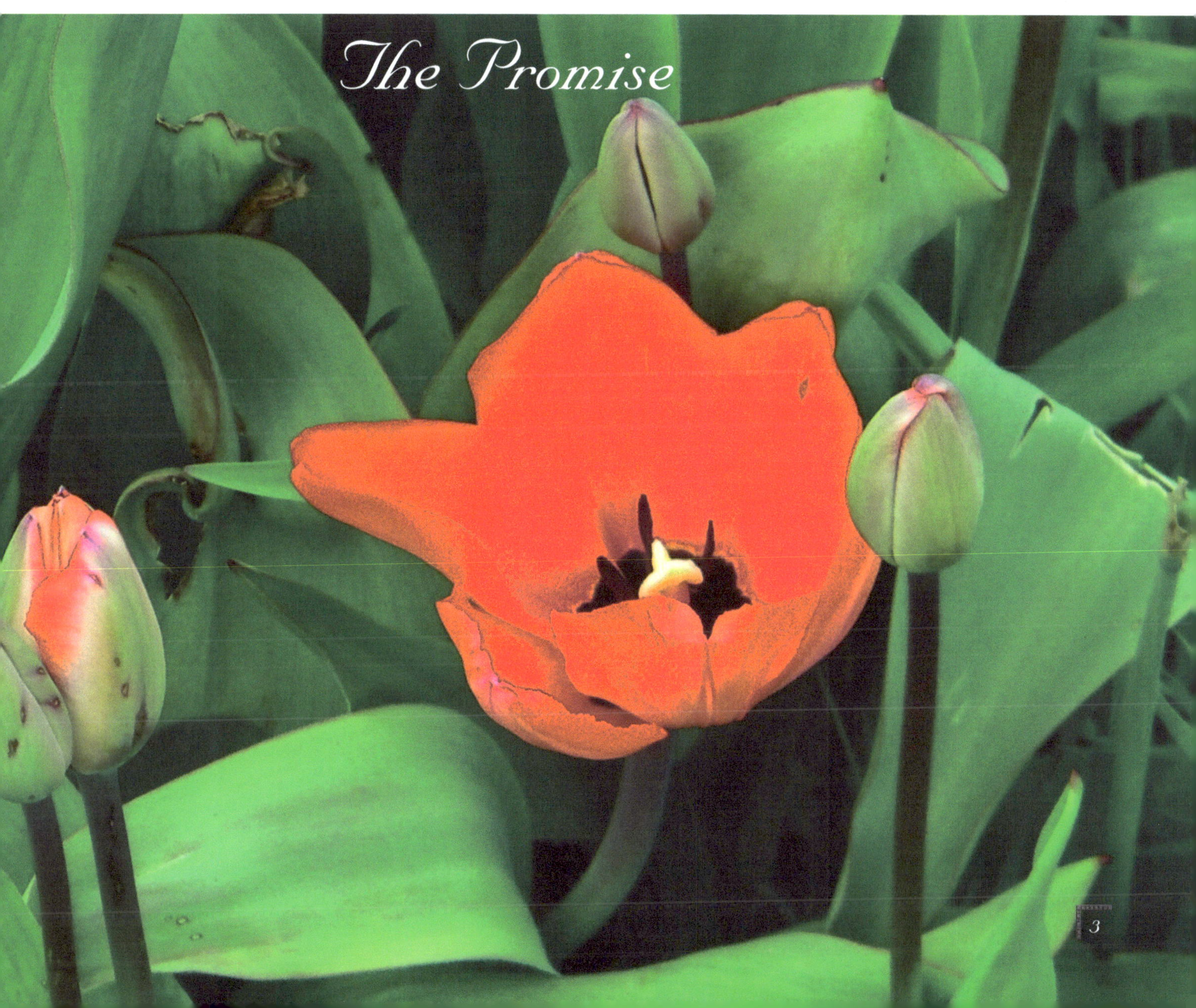

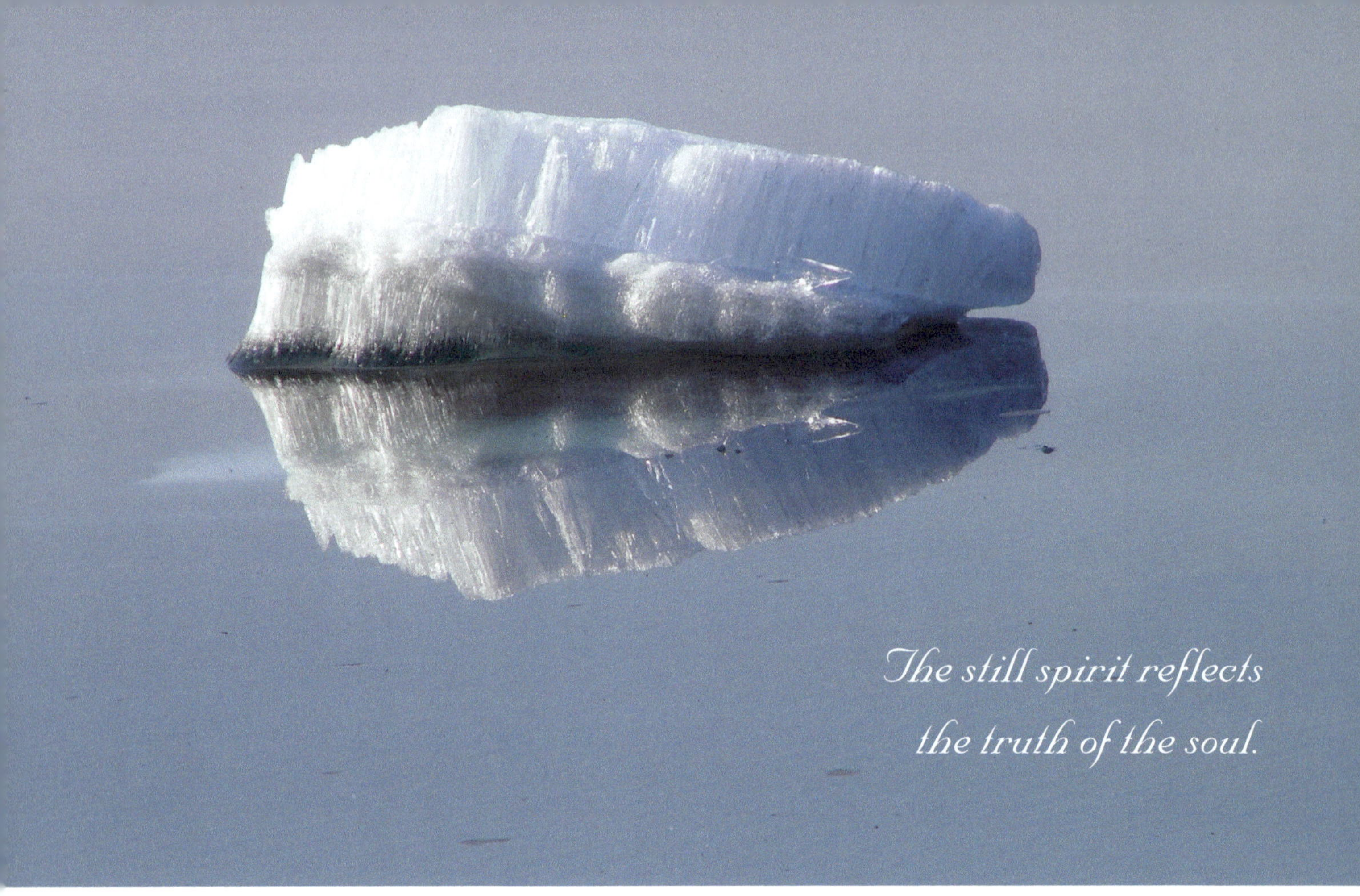

The absolute flat stillness of the lake causes a mirror-like reflection of the iceberg, crystal clear and true. When we find a place where our lives become absolutely still we can look in that stillness and see the crystal clear truth of what we hold in our soul.

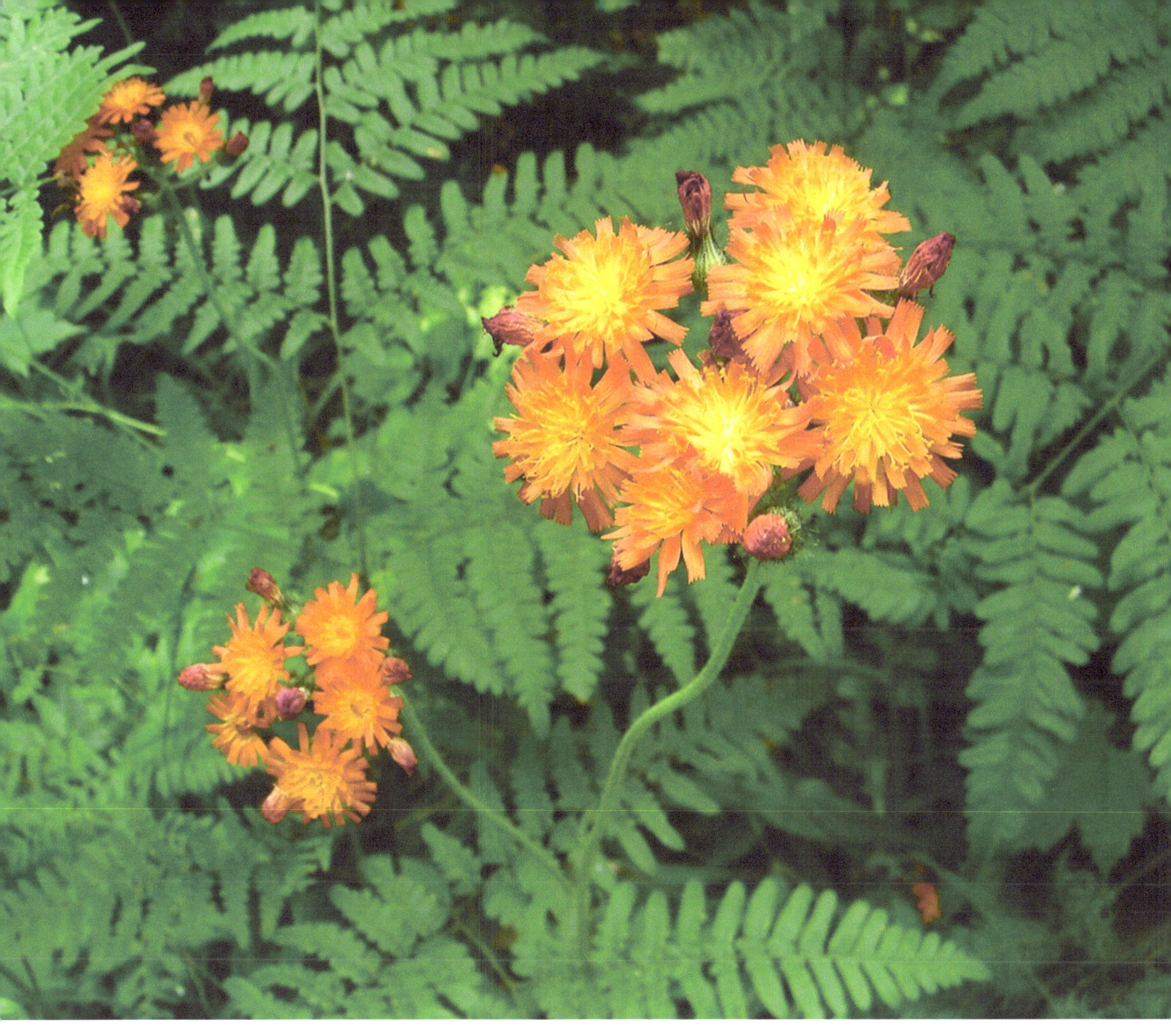

An expression of the light of the Creator's love.

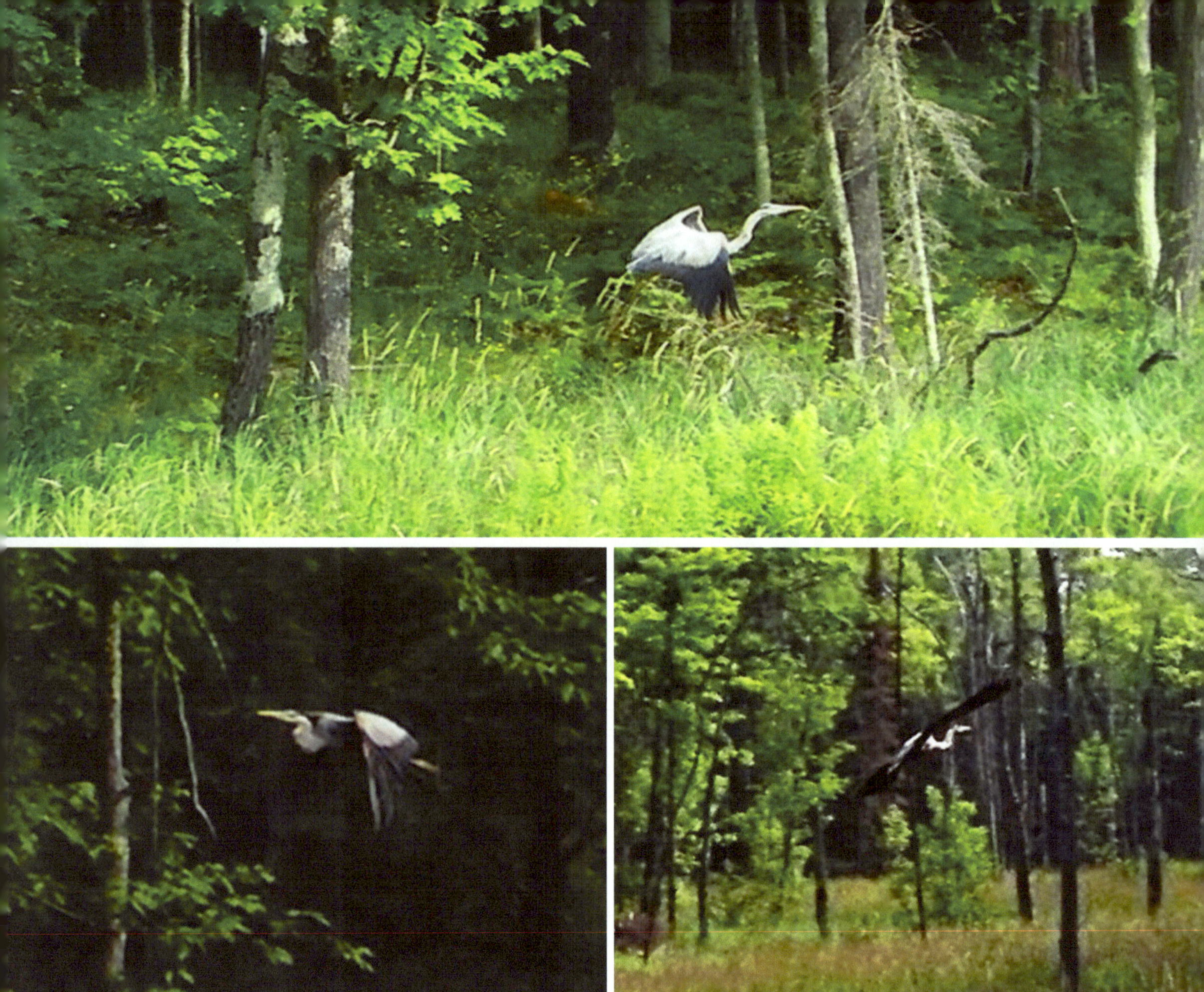

Blue Heron in Flight

(had to act fast!!!)

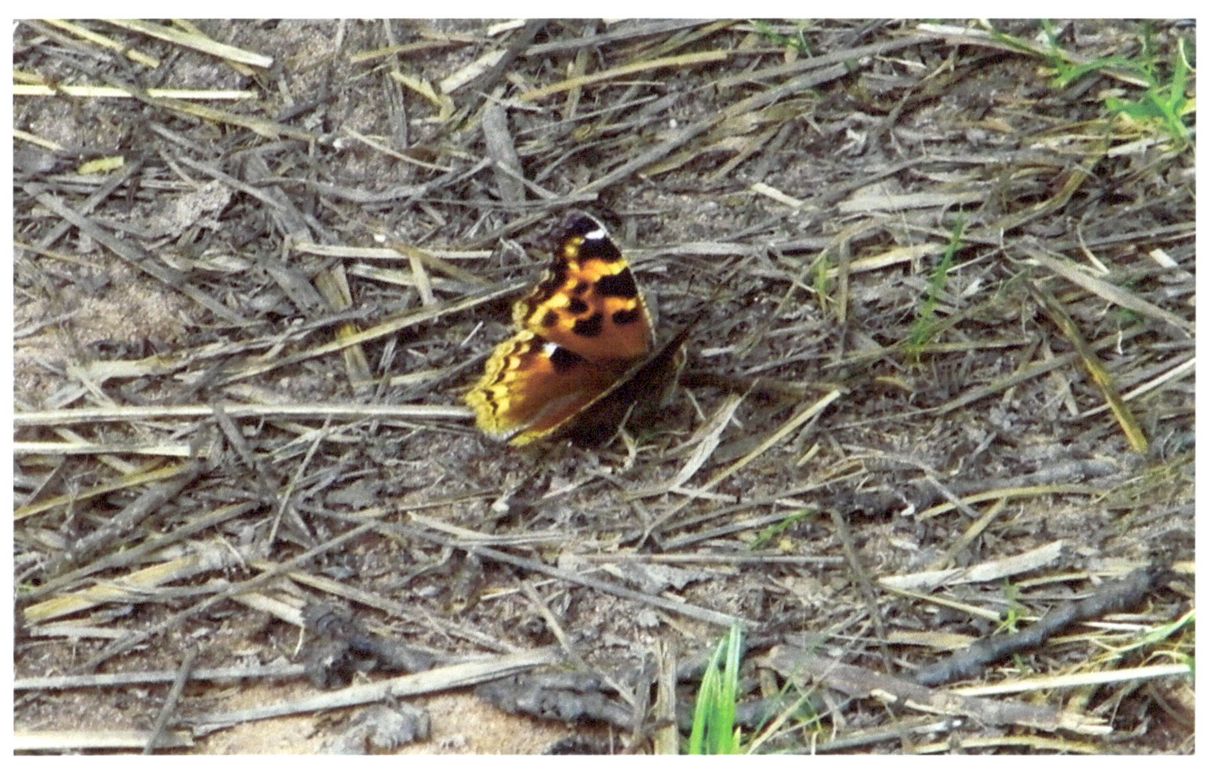

God paints some of His brightest colors

on some of His humblest creatures.

Laughter Factory!

The happiest of flowers ...

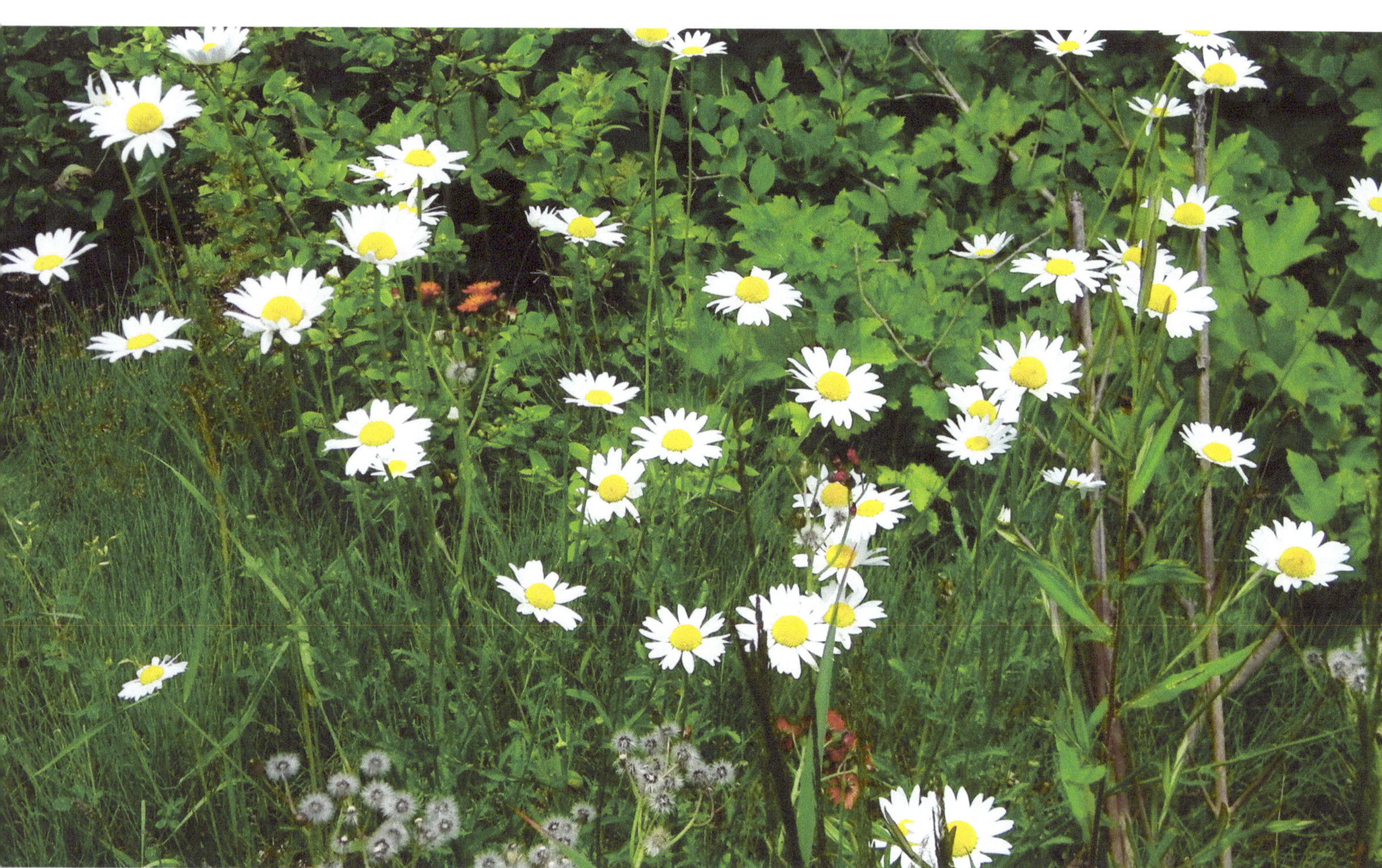

God provides safety for all

as the spider fades into the white camouflage of the daisy's petals.

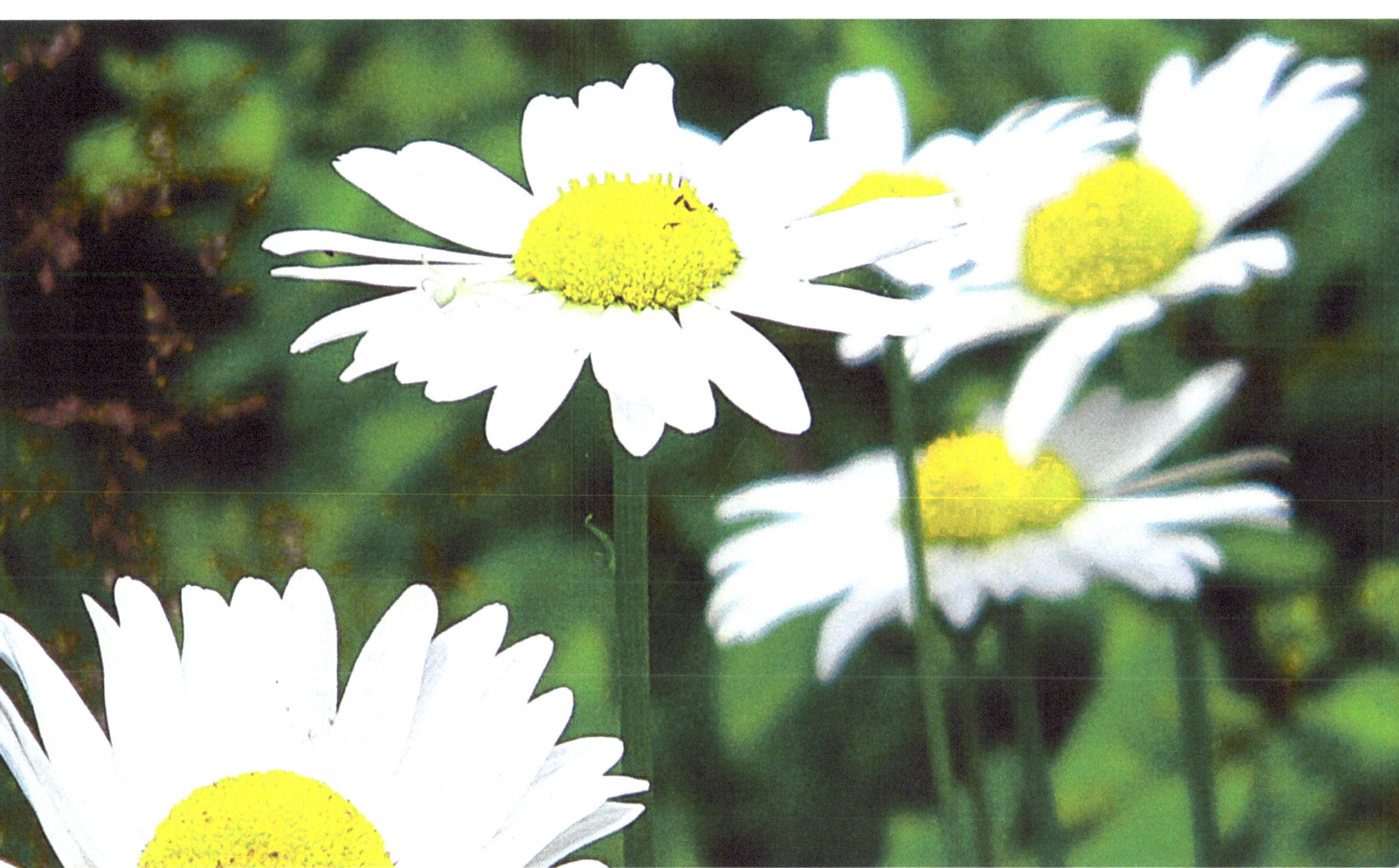

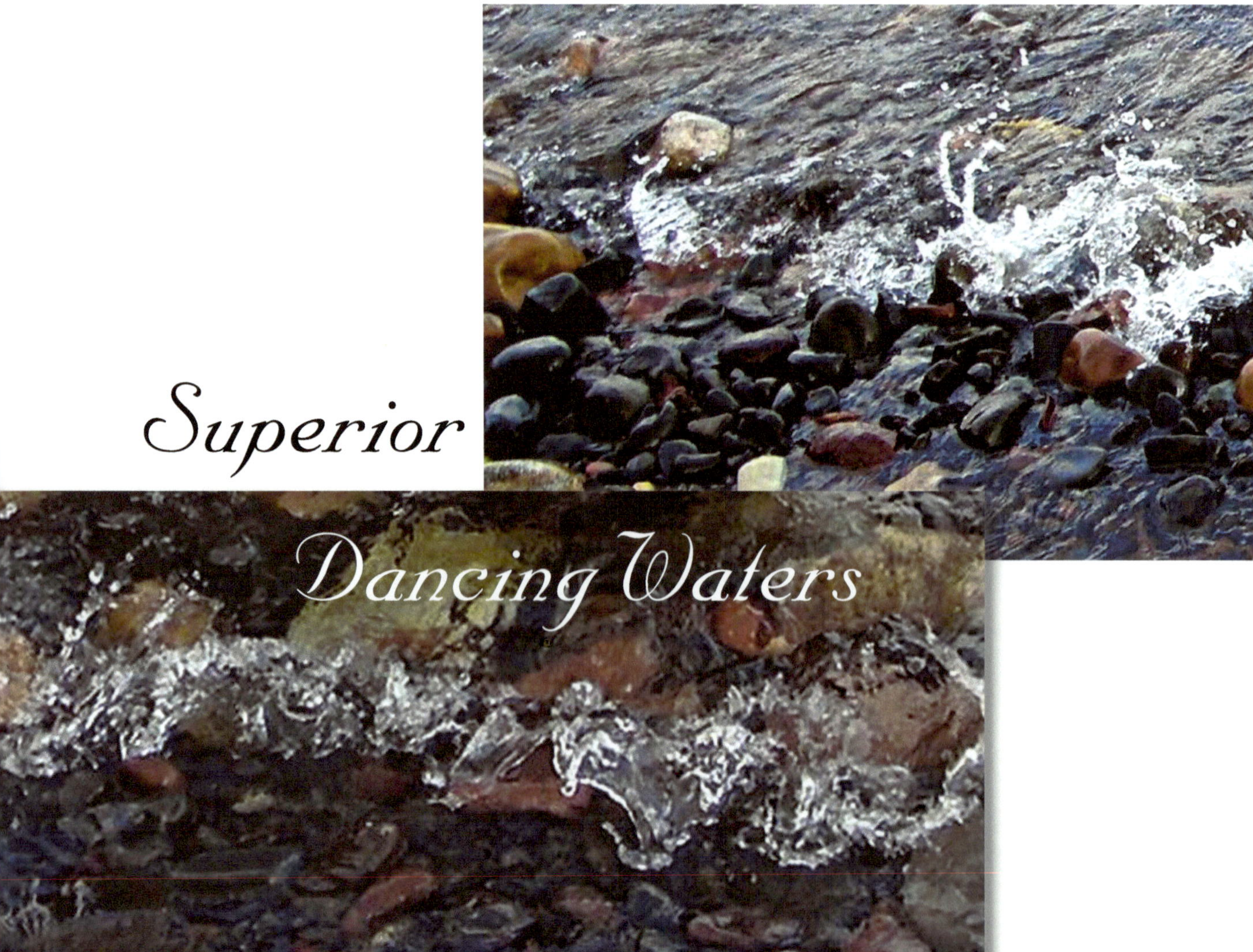

Superior

Dancing Waters

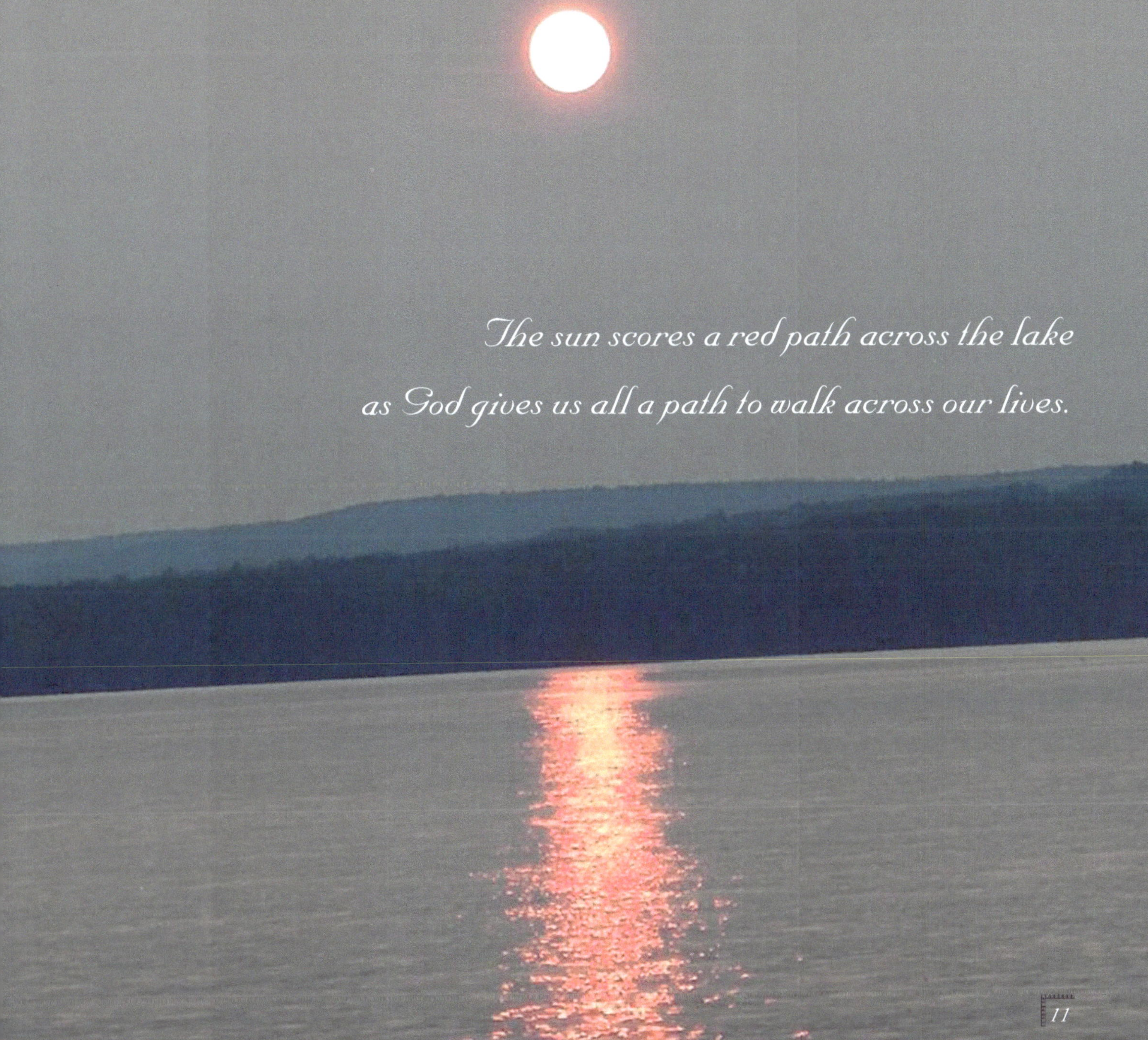

The sun scores a red path across the lake
as God gives us all a path to walk across our lives.

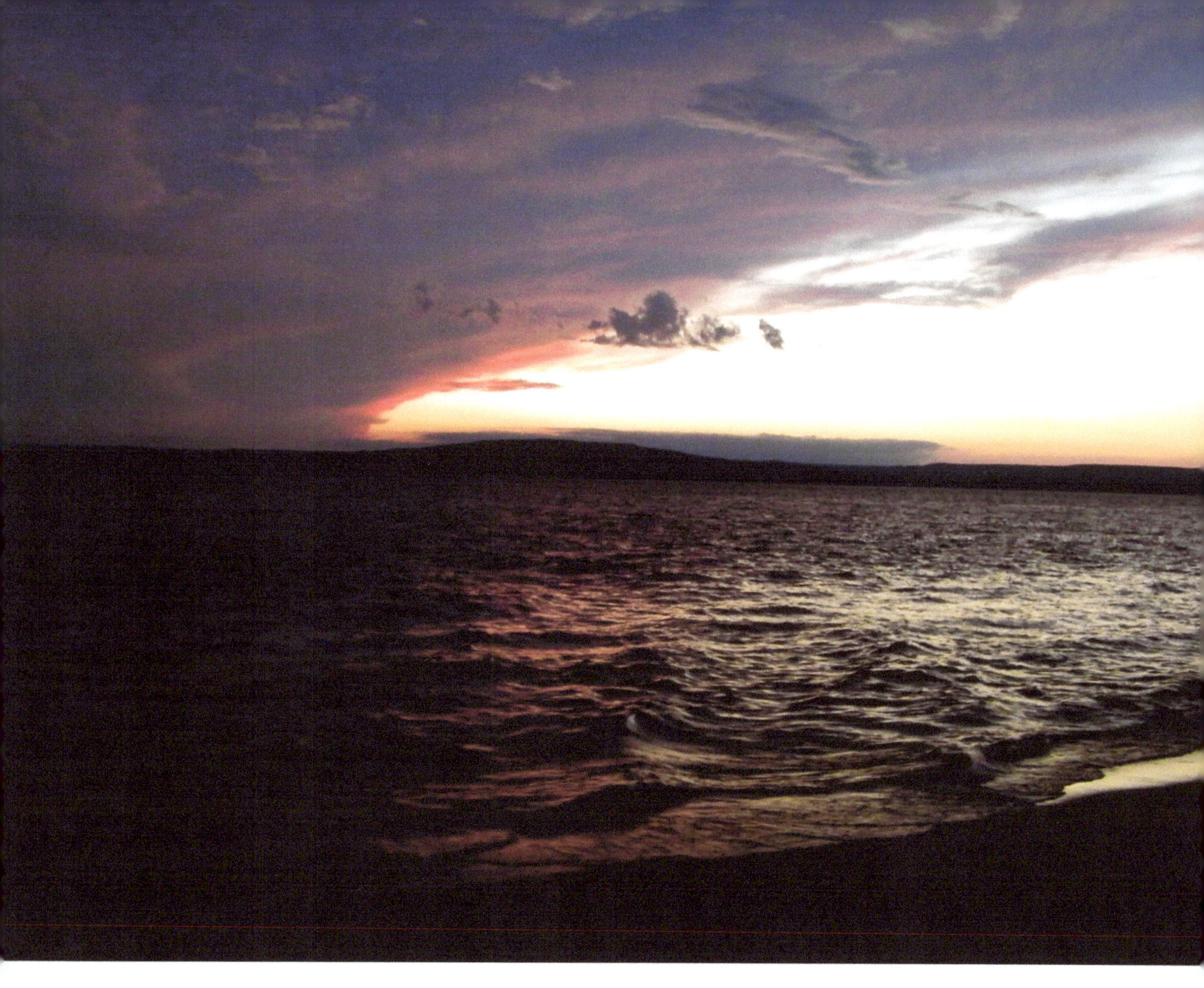

A sunset from Grant's Point

Grant's Point in high summer colors -

lush green and brilliant blue and clean white

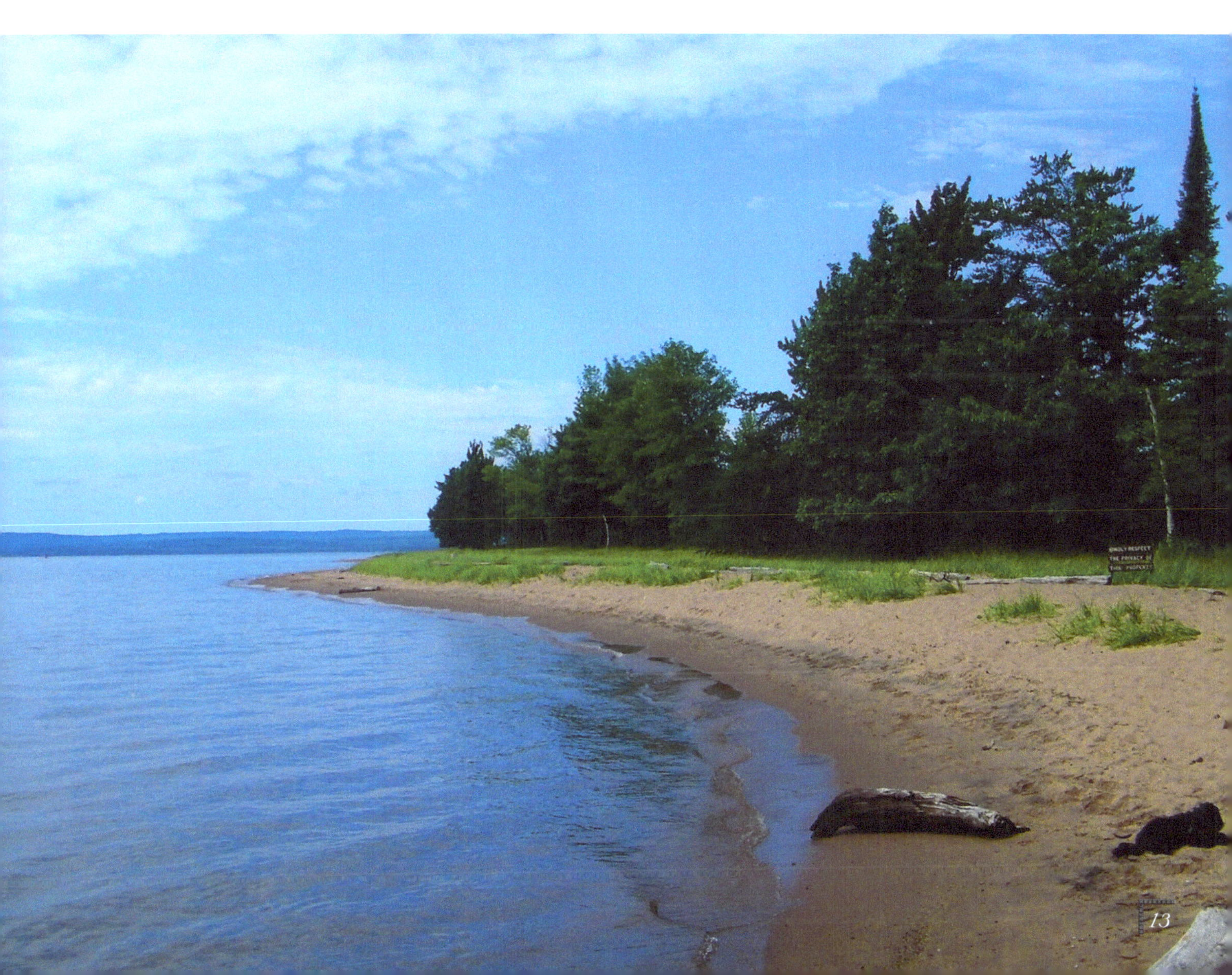

August Full Moon

Connspaid Gealach

Gaelic: Dispute Moon

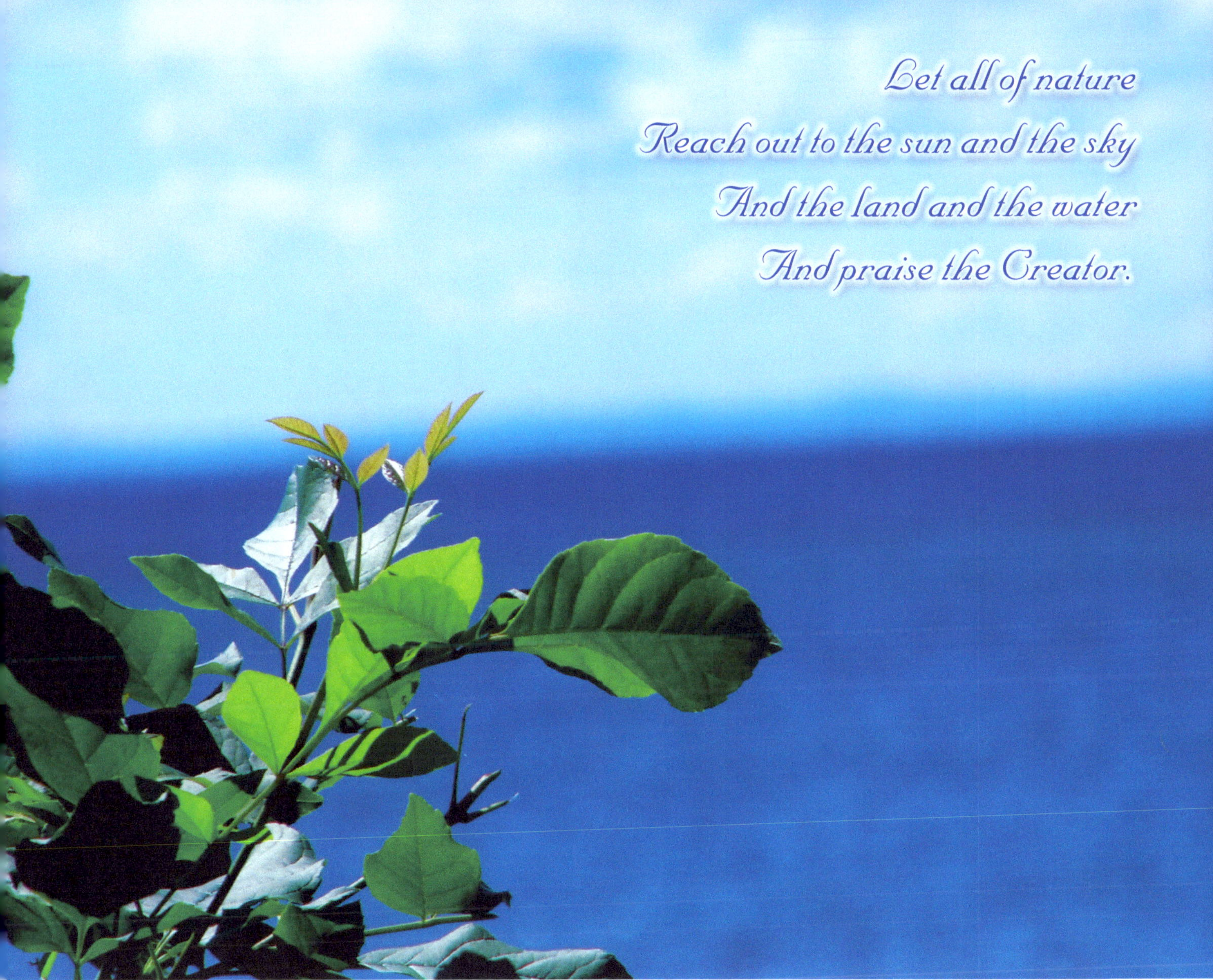

I was supposedly taking a picture of the lake but my camera had other ideas. When I checked on the shots for the day here was this perfectly focused photo of these little sprouts clearly reaching out to the sun and for all the world cheering "Hey Dad! This is Great!!" And so the verse was written.

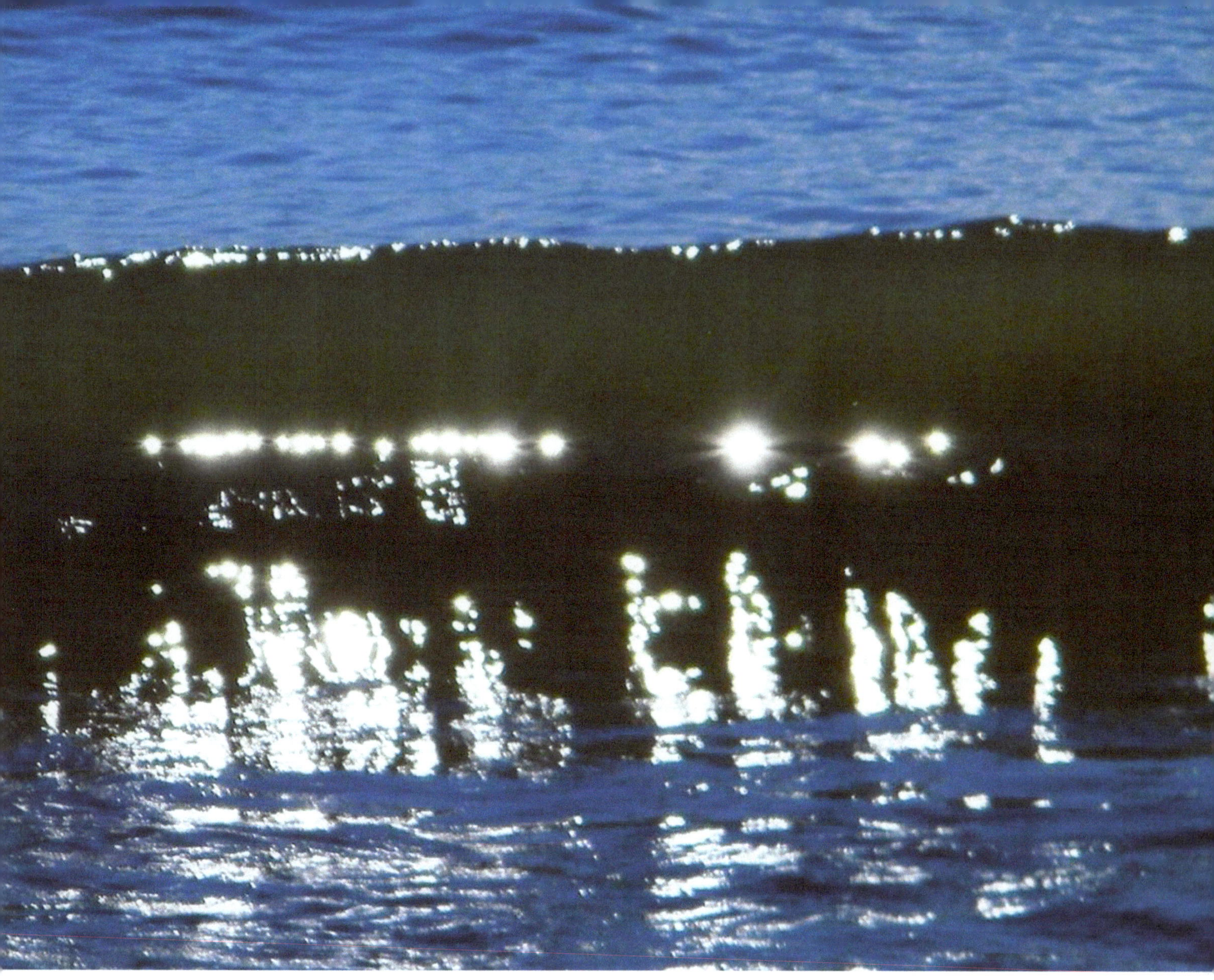

Was shooting for breaking waves to catch the interesting creatures that show up in the froth.

But this wave seemed to wait just that moment to be caught, as if forever in that place of

just before breaking.

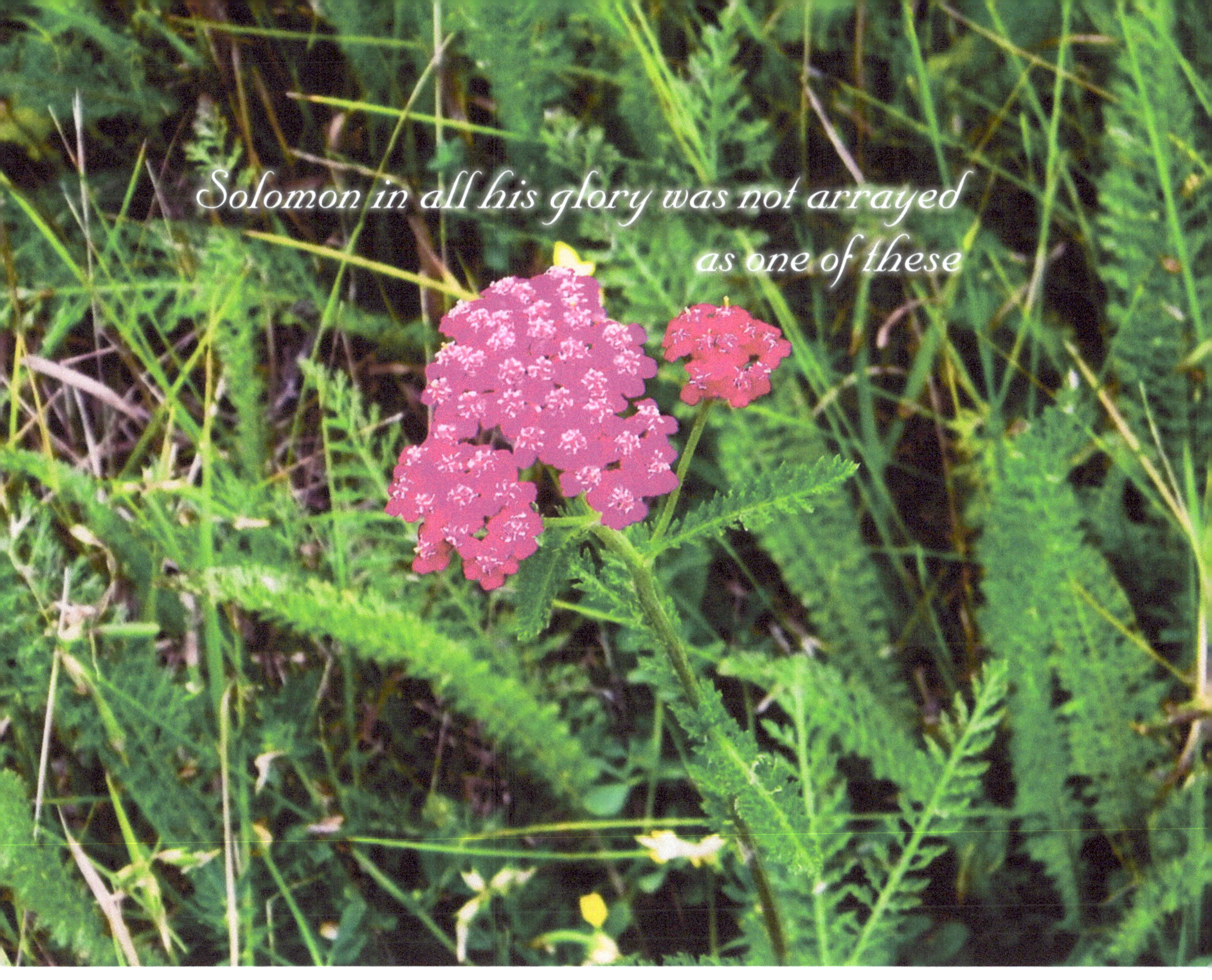

A Lily of the Field

From the Sermon on the Mount

Matthew 6:29 and Luke 12:27

The Legend of the Woodland Ship

There is a story of a huge ship that looks just like an island but it sails the inland seas of the world. It is manned by trees and animals and all manner of living creatures. And it is captained by ...

Well, we'll have to wait and see. For in this picture the trees, the officers, standing straight and tall at attention on either side of the boarding platform, await their captain who is about to climb up the side of the ship from the launch below.

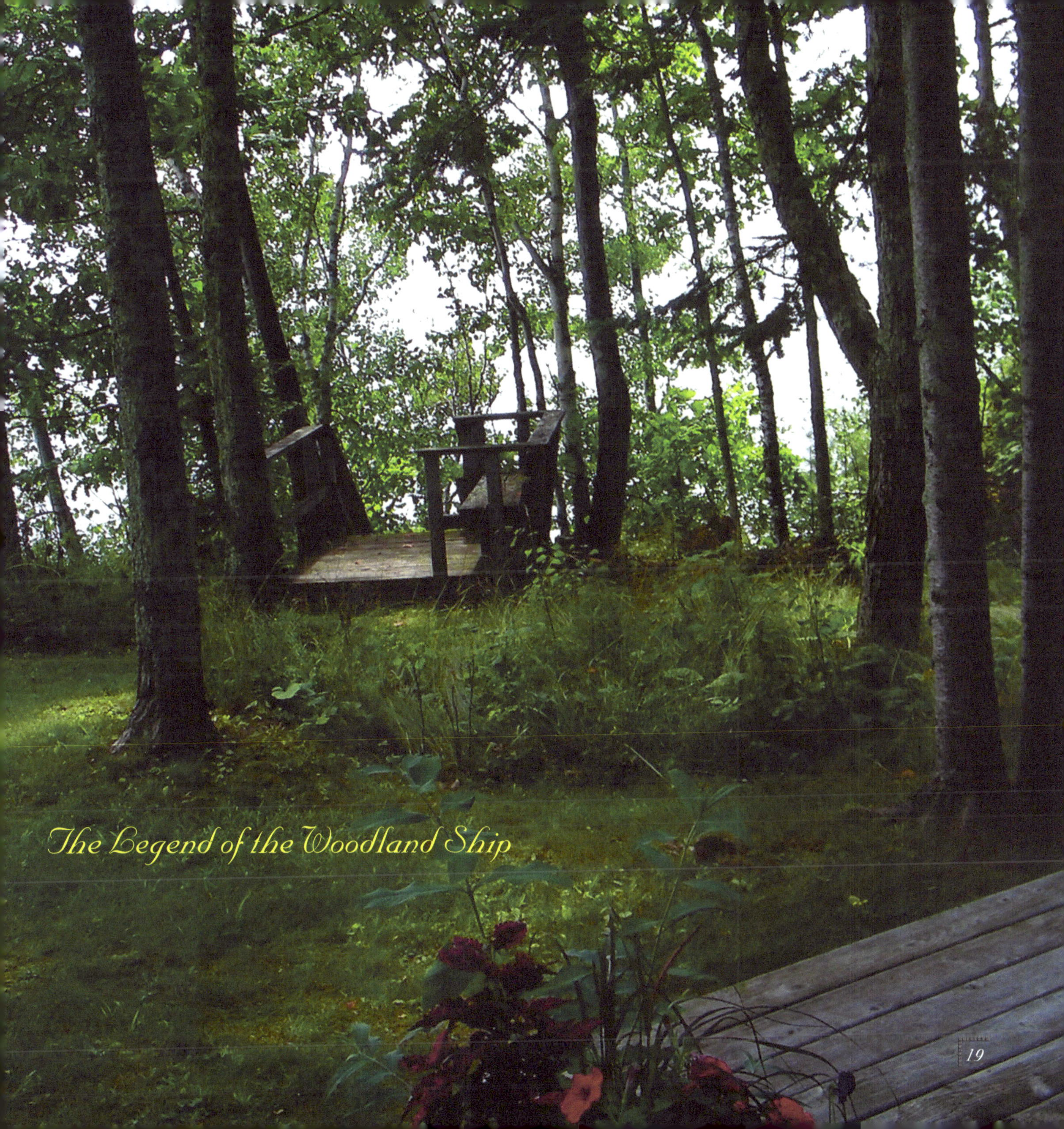
The Legend of the Woodland Ship

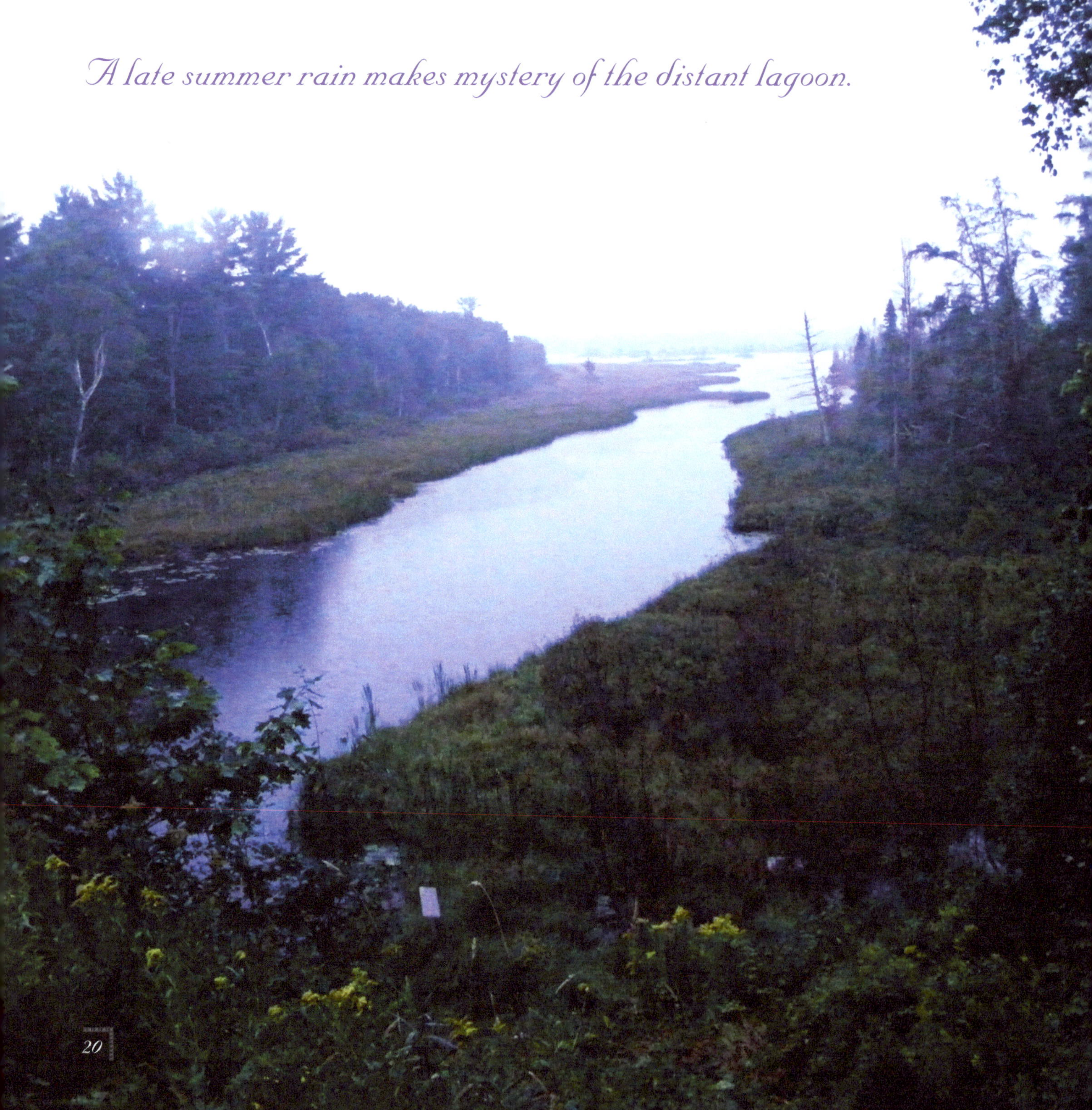

A late summer rain makes mystery of the distant lagoon.

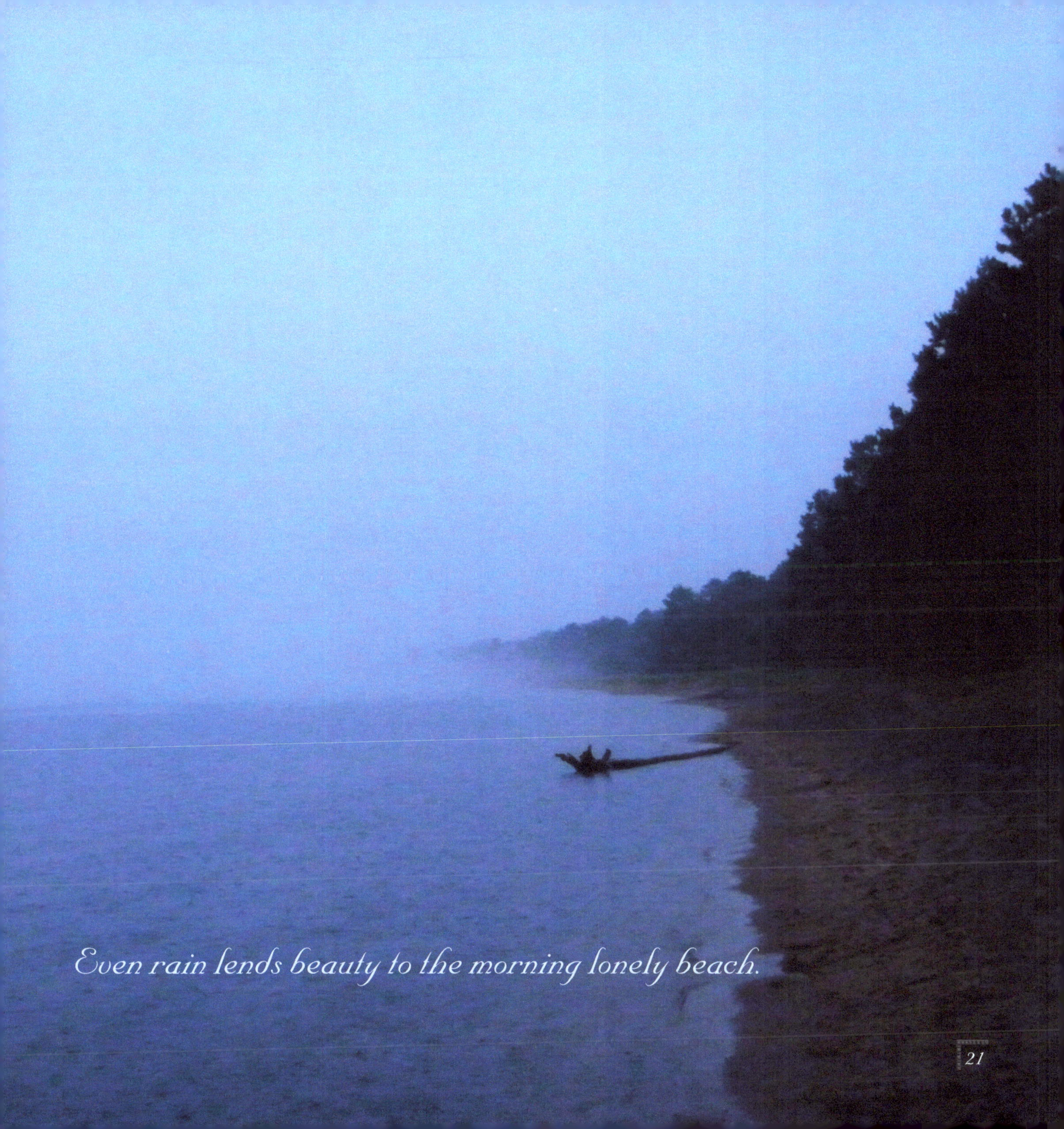

Even rain lends beauty to the morning lonely beach.

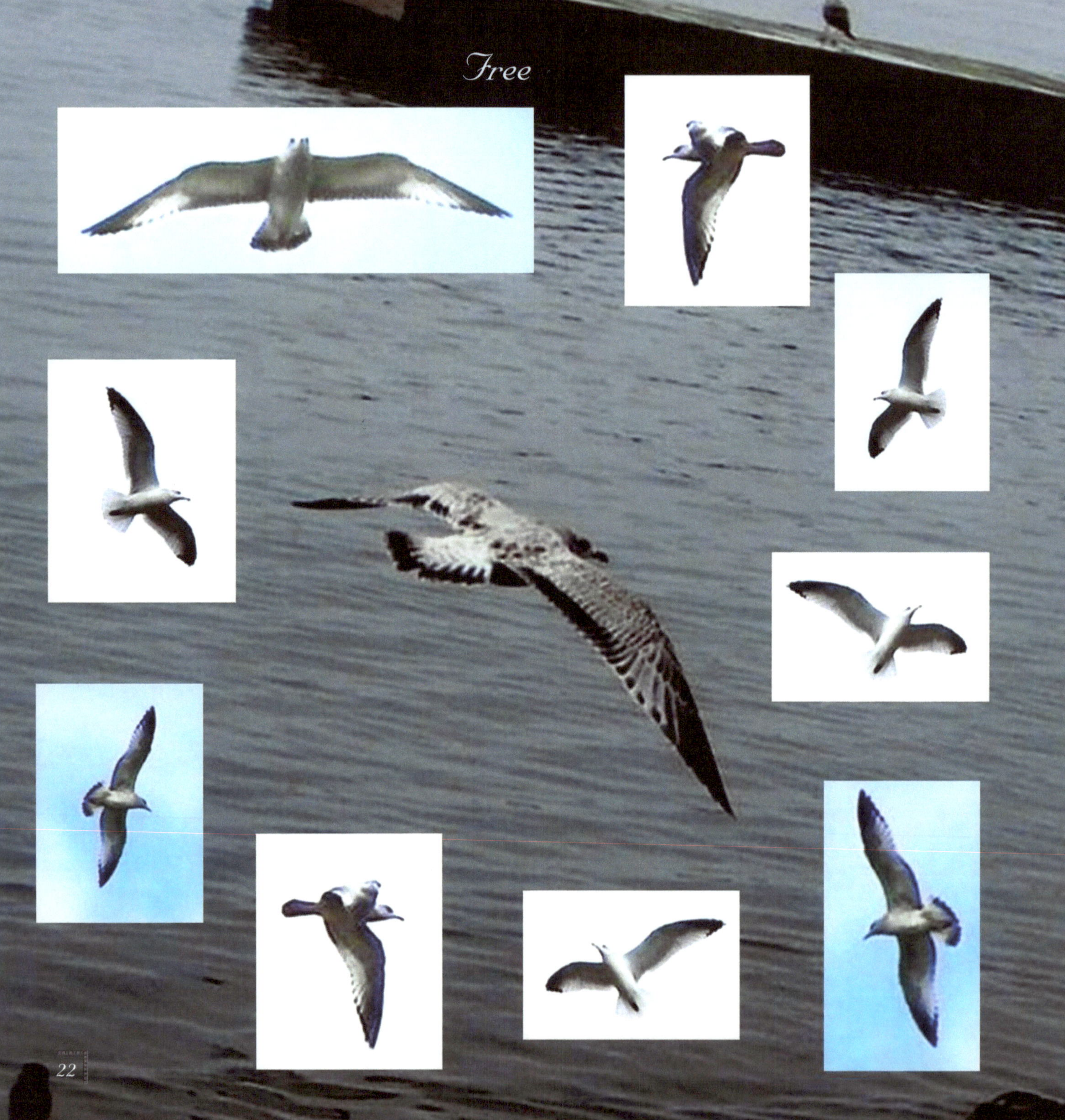

Free

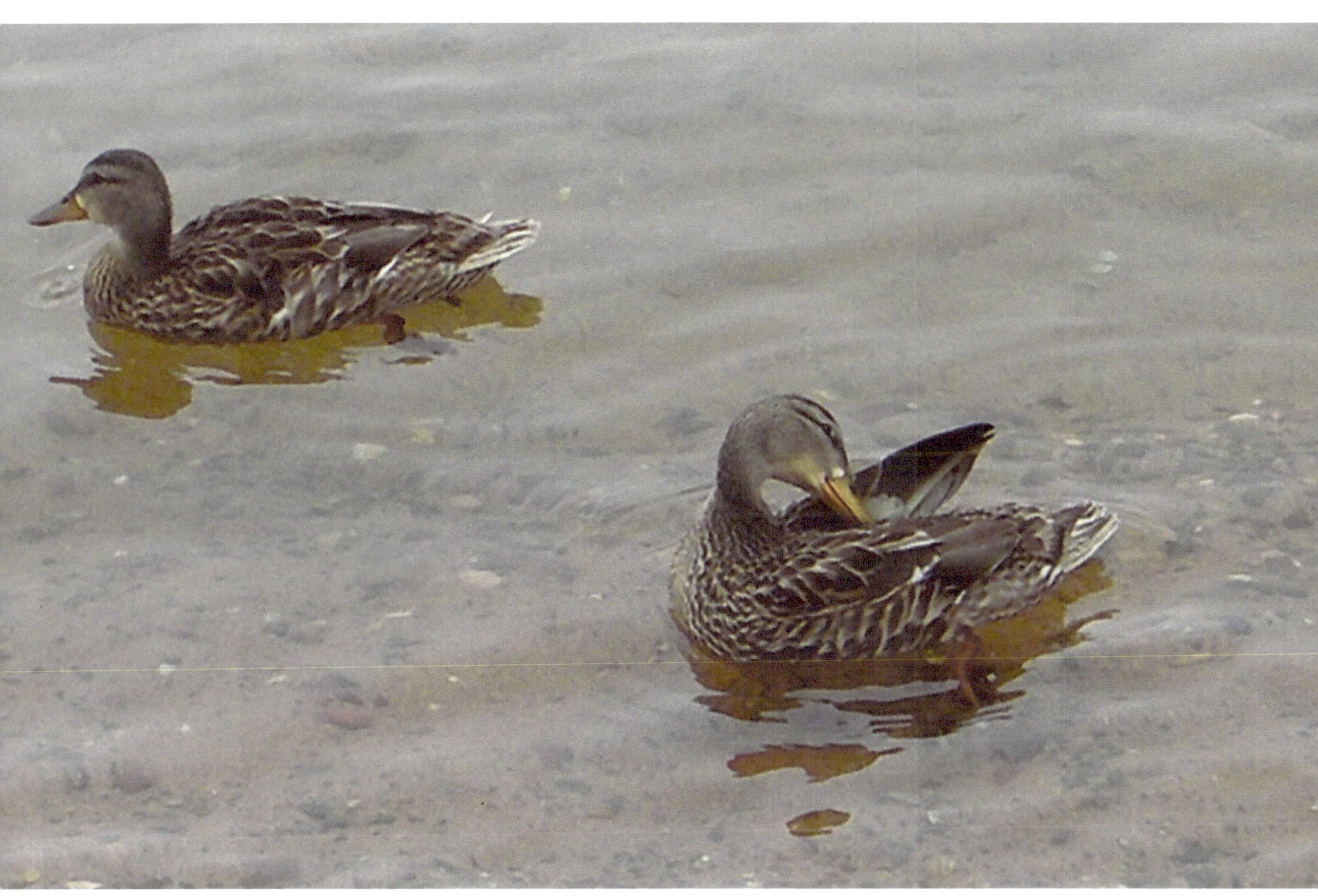

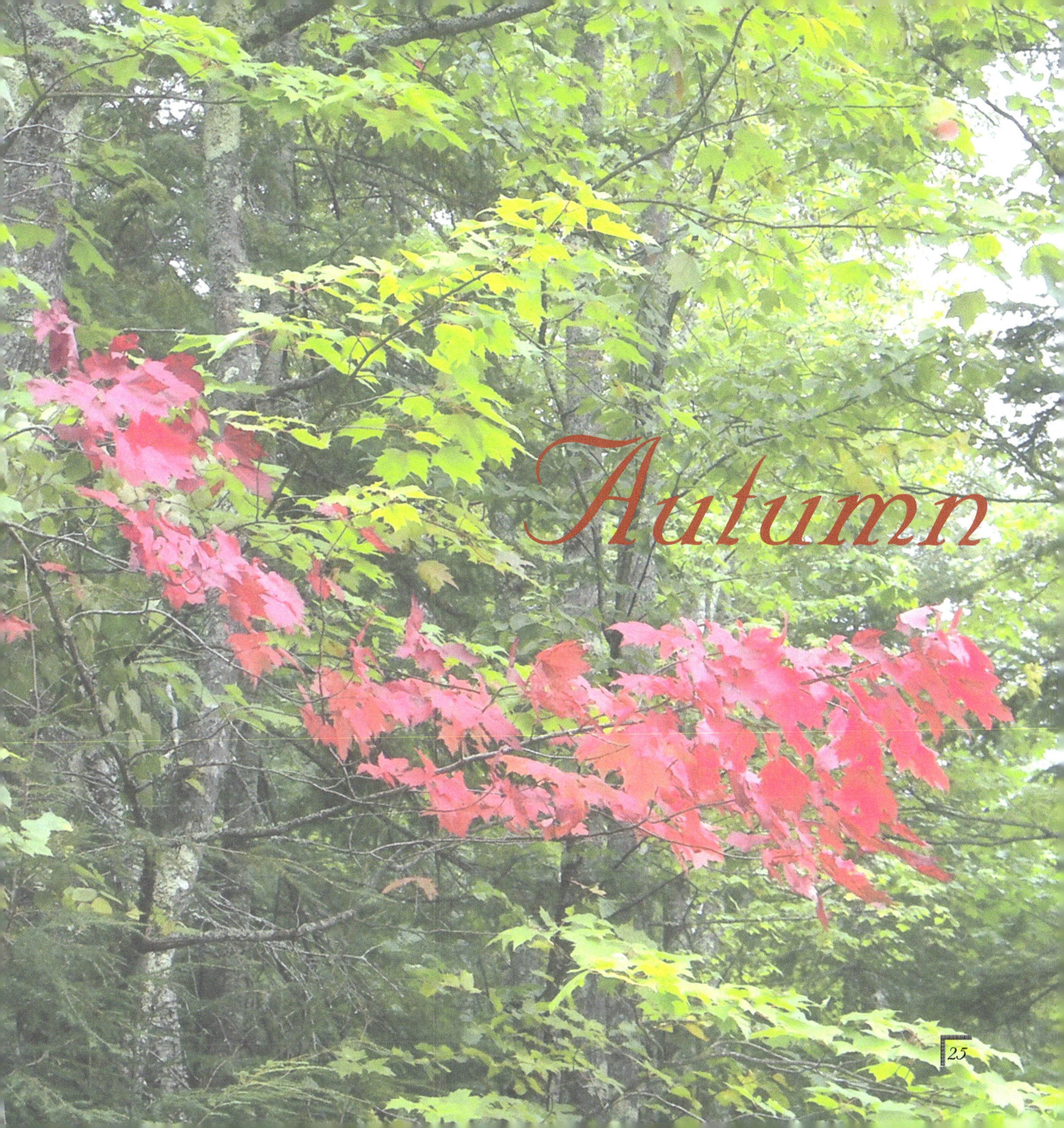
Autumn

Transition. Change. All part of the cycle of life.

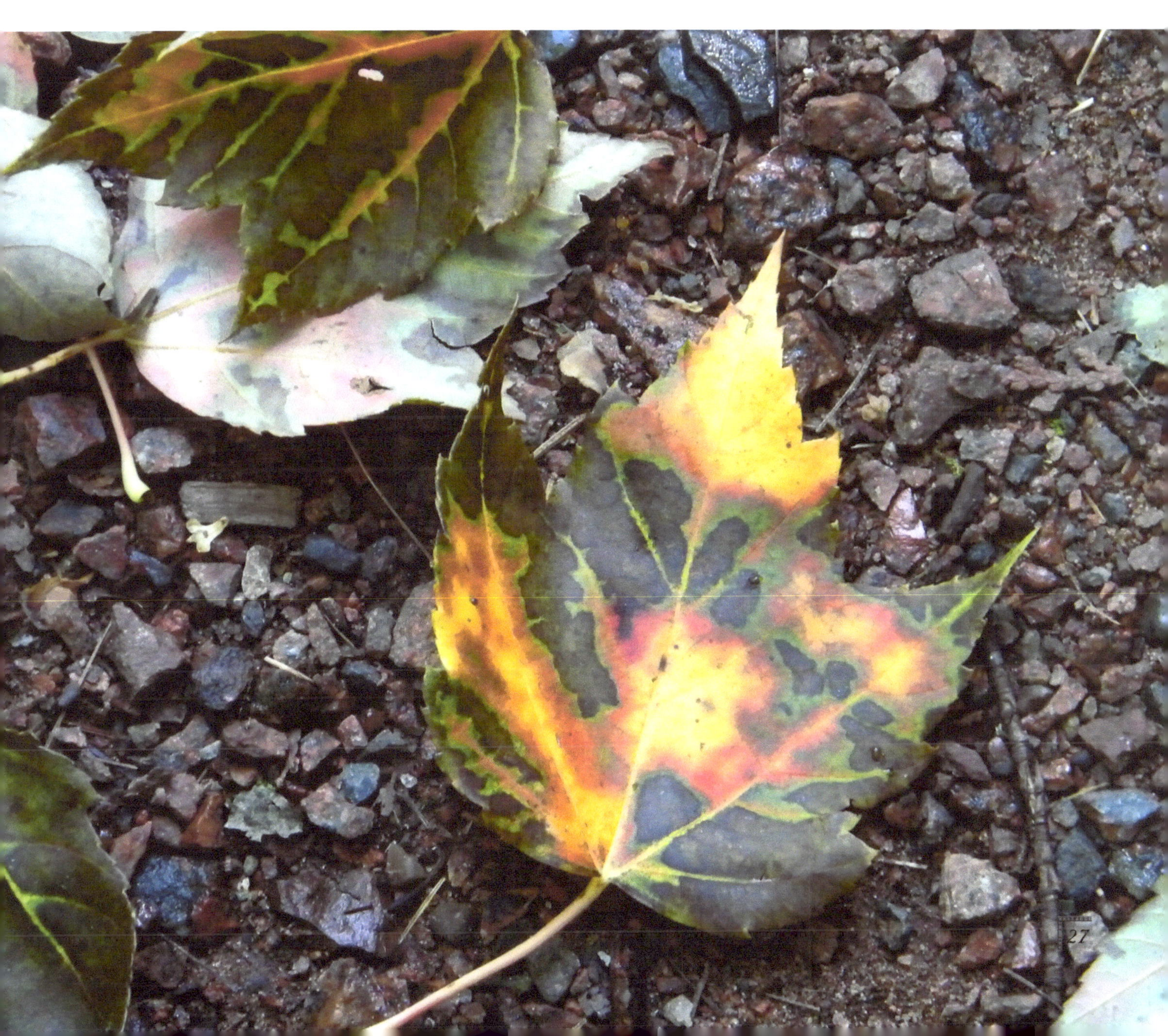

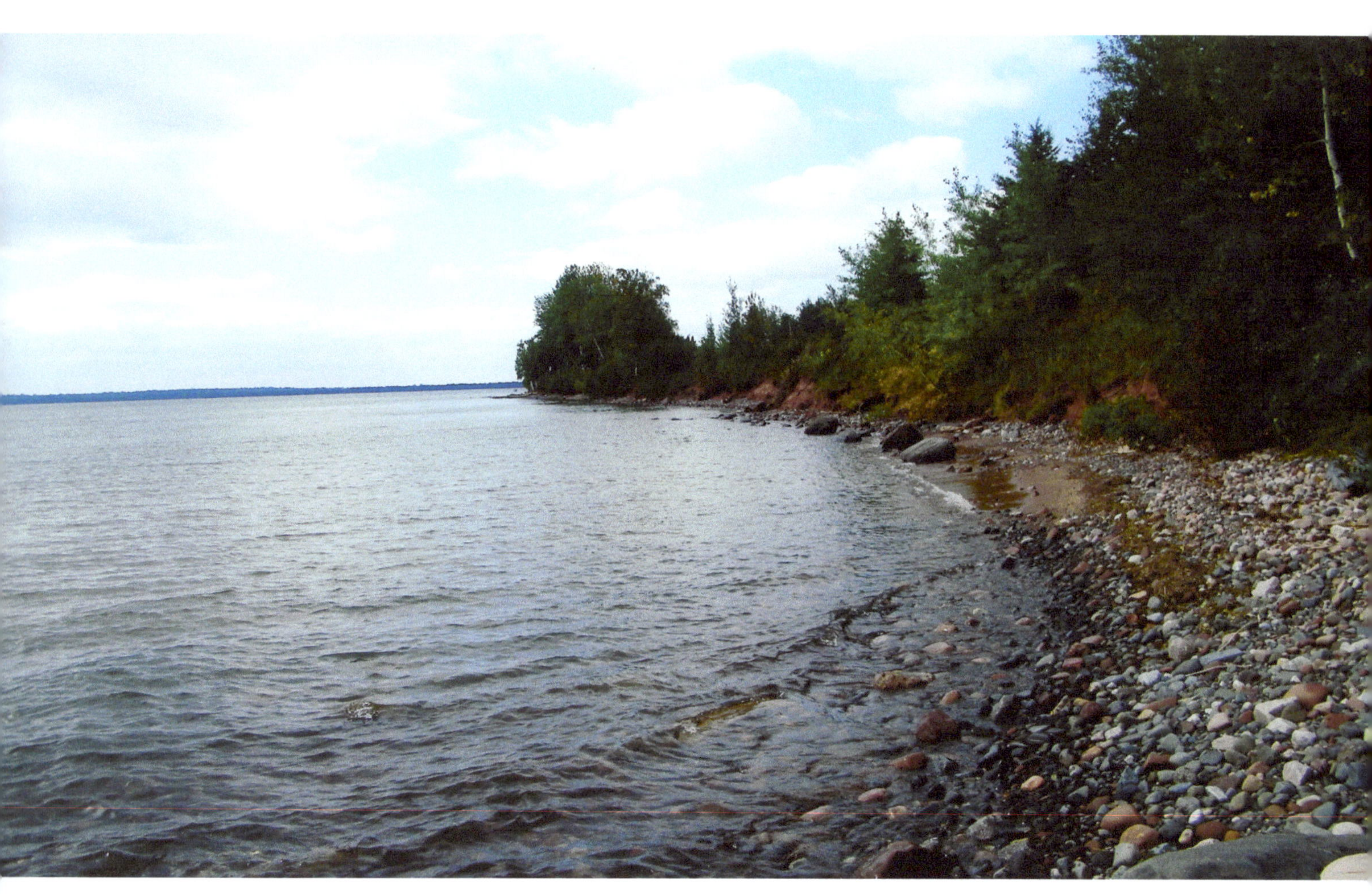

Peace reigns on this shore.

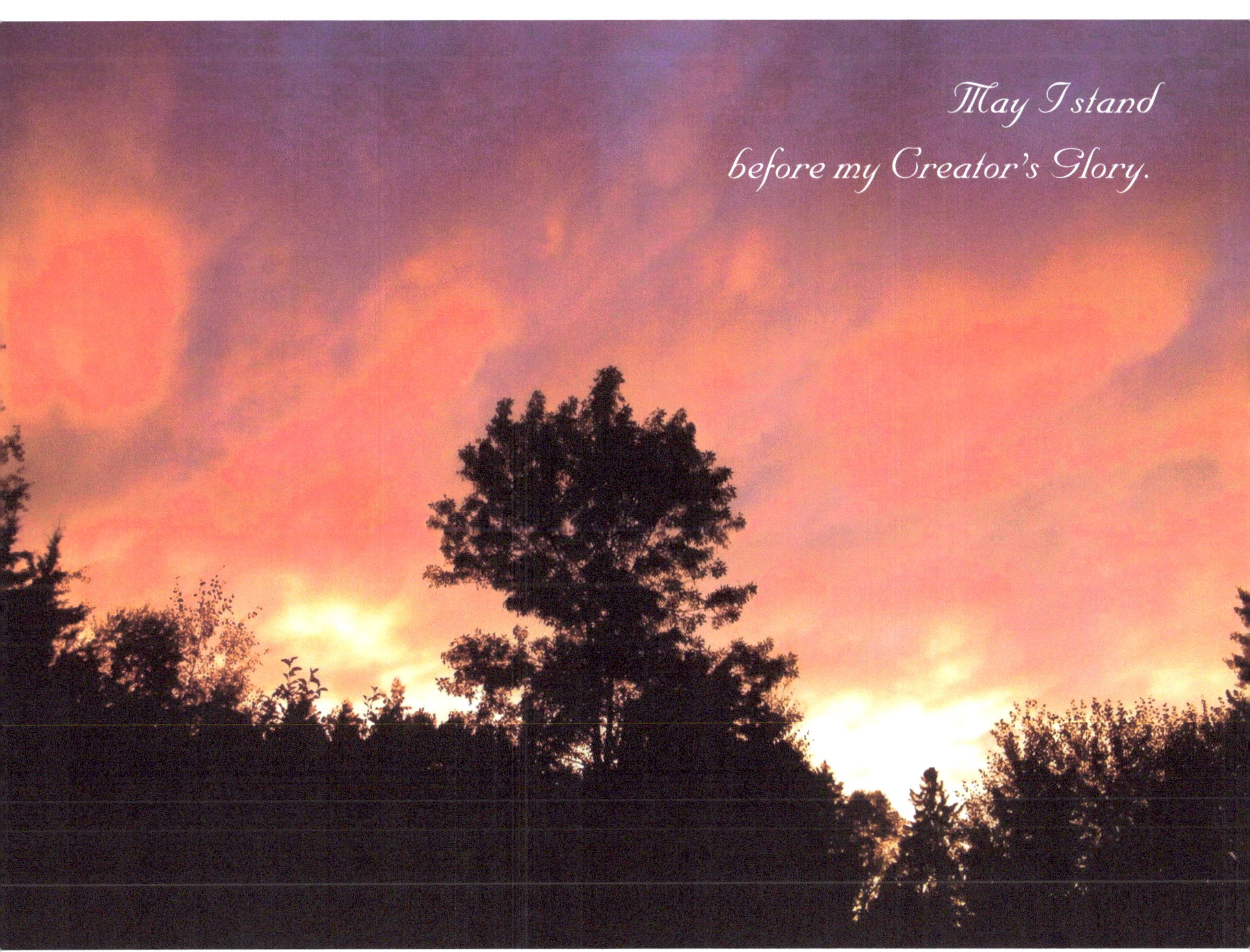
May I stand
before my Creator's Glory.

Deer, bear, coyote, wolf, hawk, eagle, crane, heron

and many more make the Island their home.

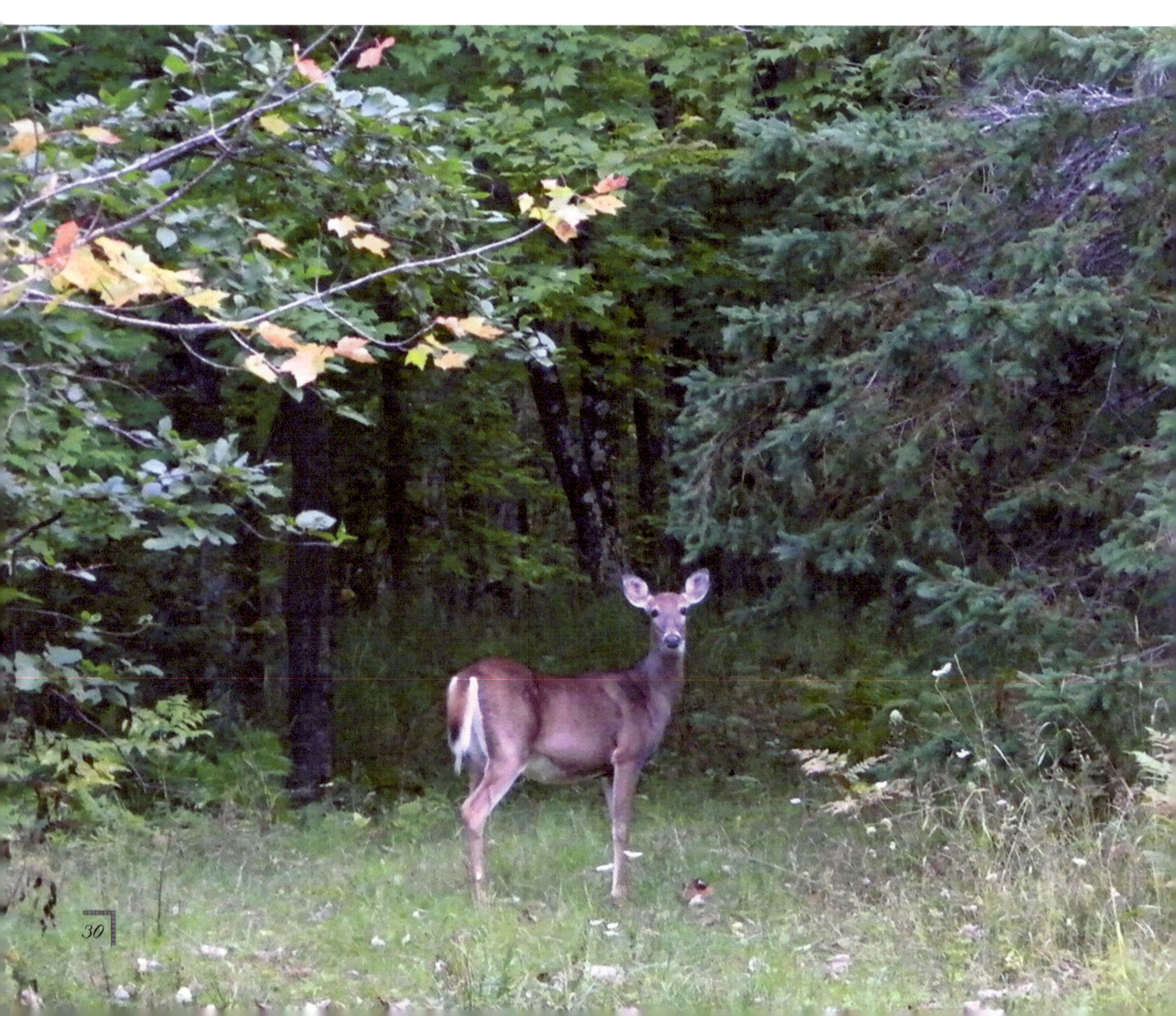

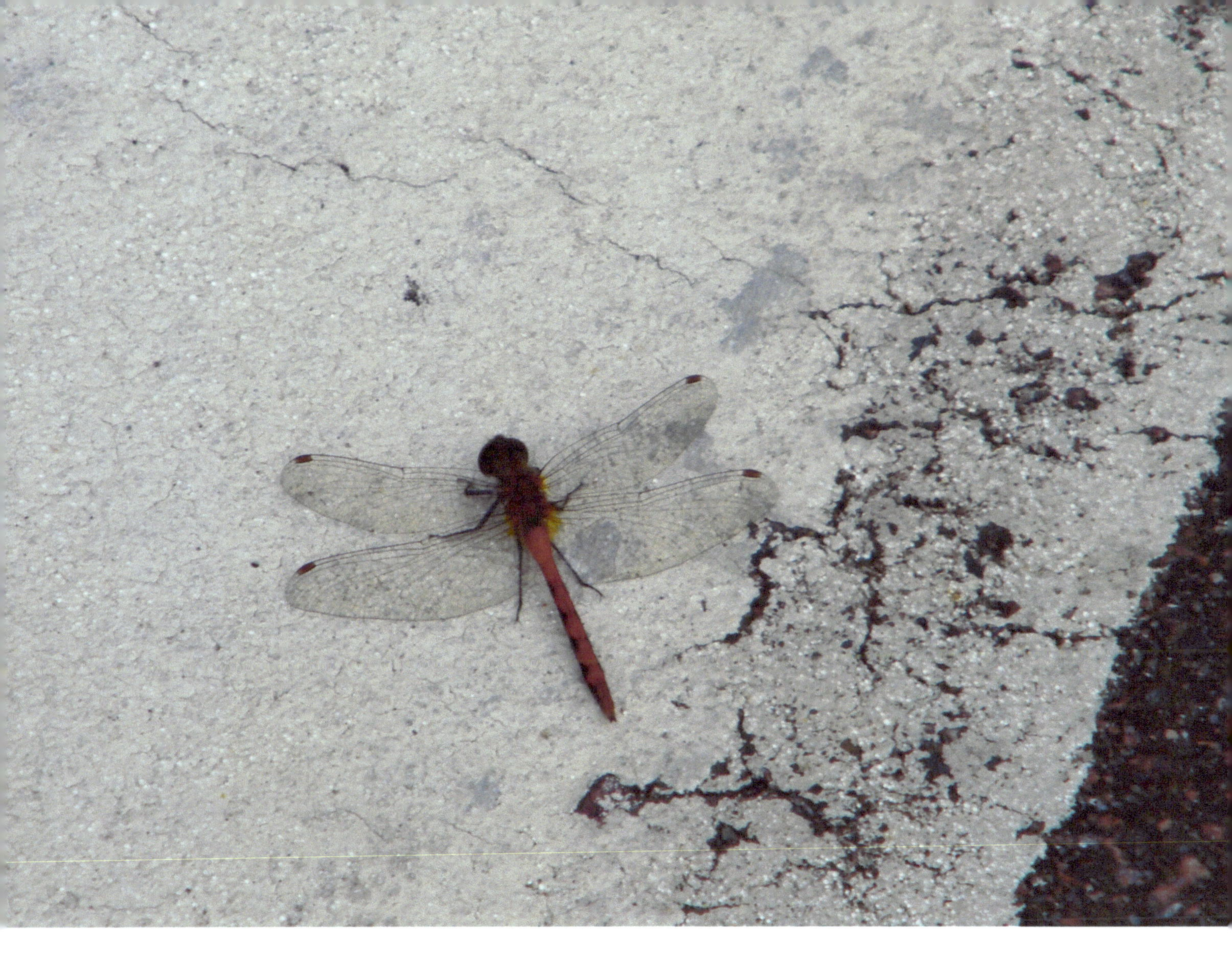

A plucky, wee fellow

was flying away a second later.

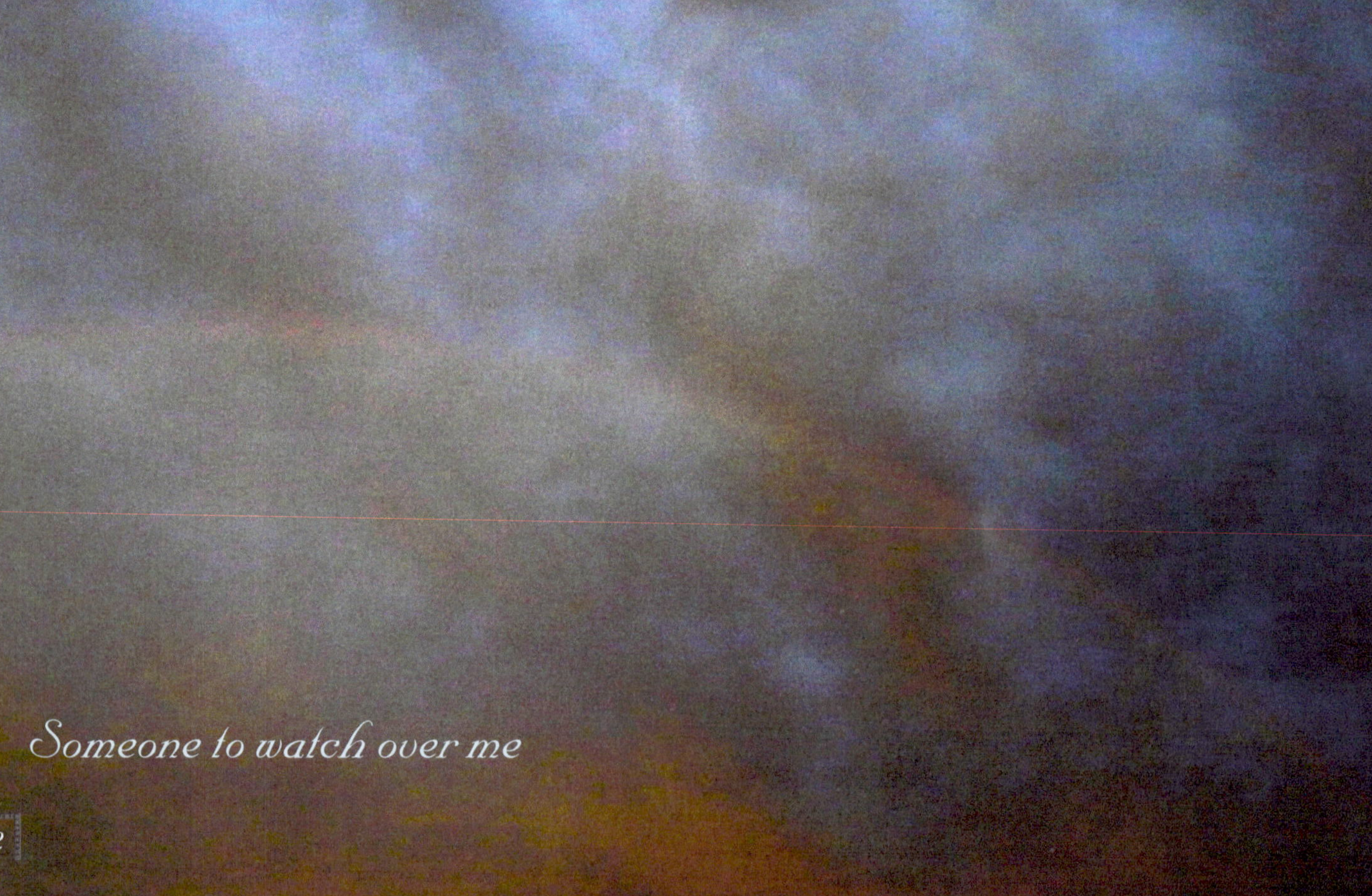

Angels appear in the most amazing places.

In trying to draw out the rainbow,

I drew out an angel.

Someone to watch over me

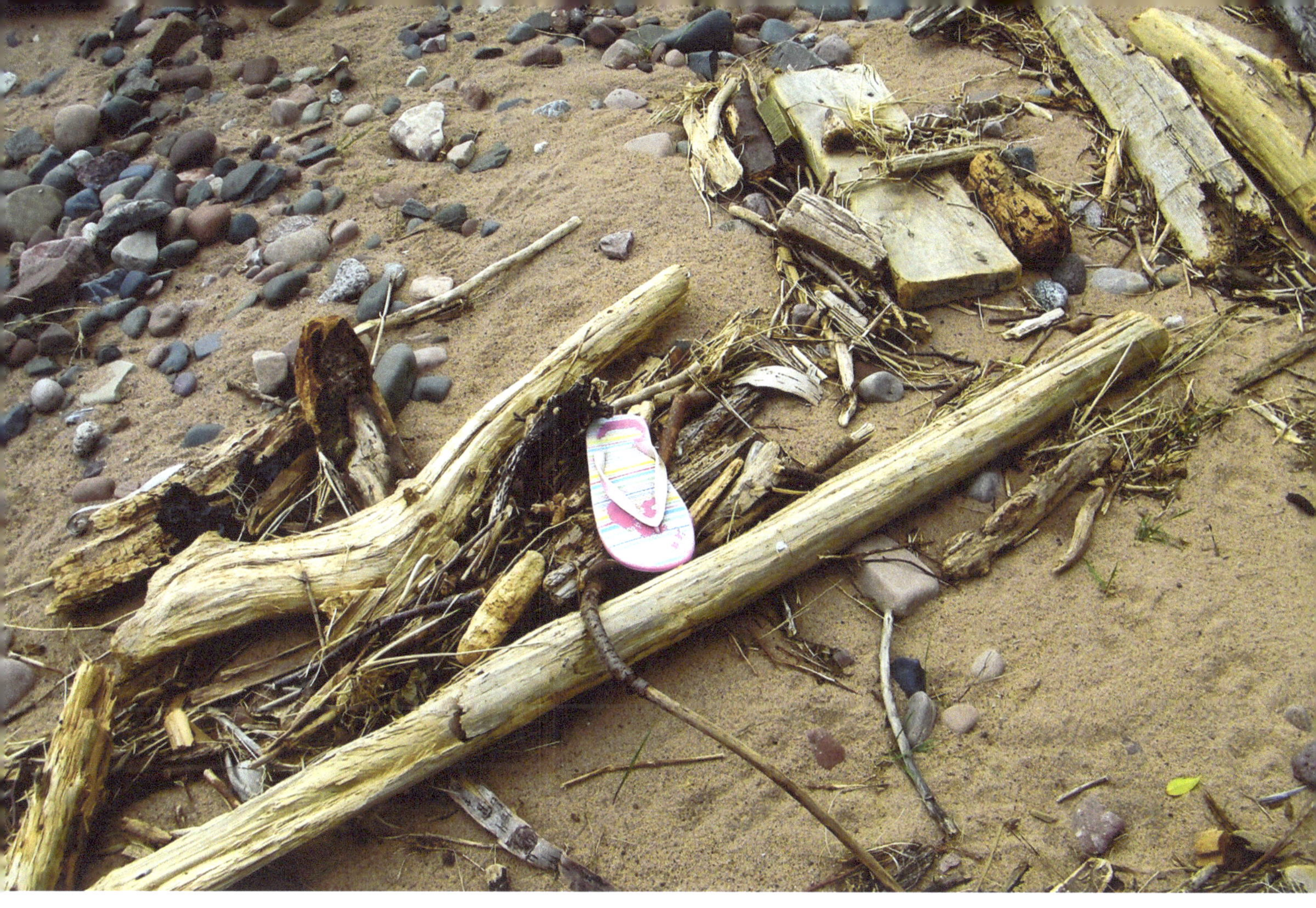

What's left after the storm.

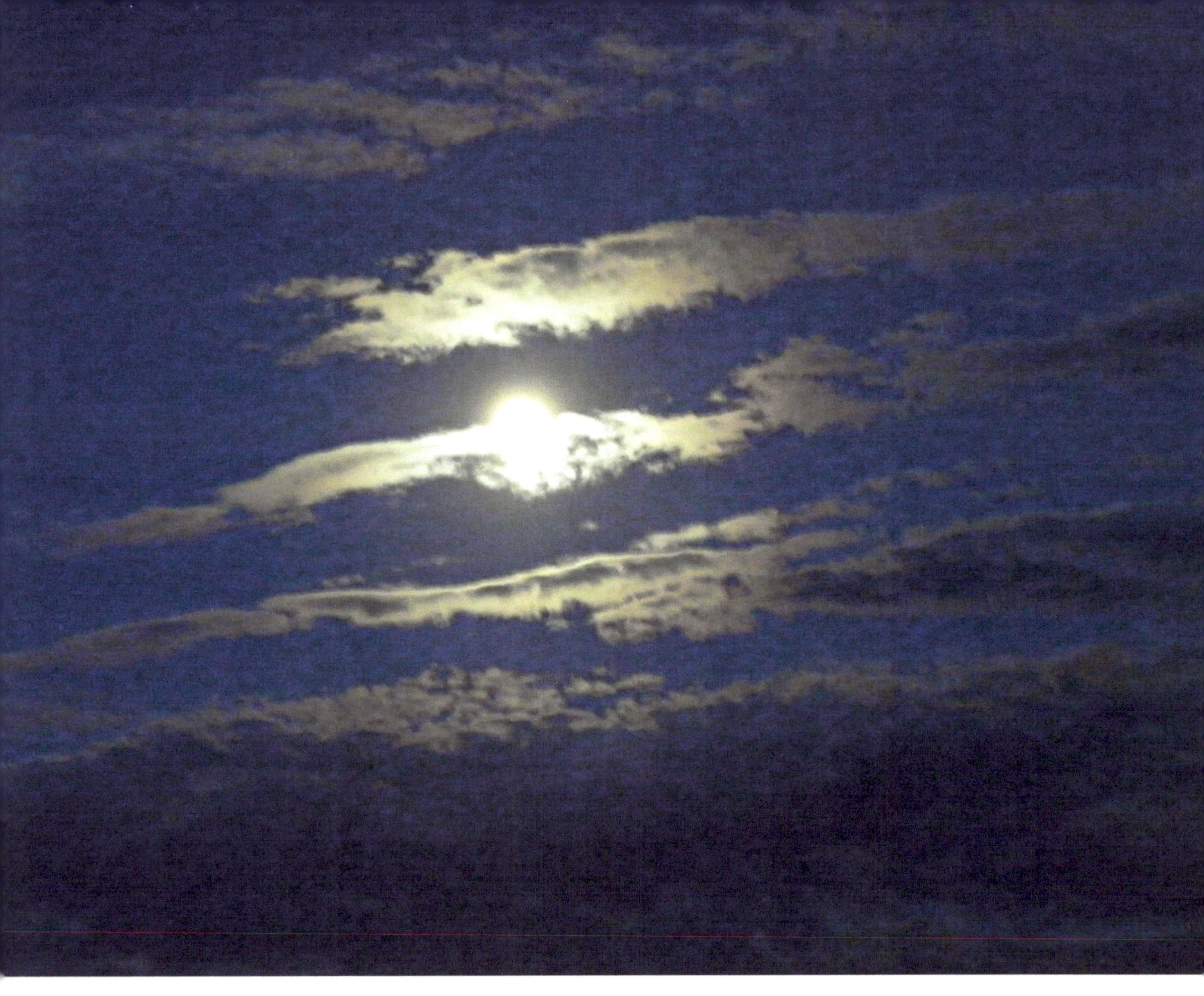

September Full Moon playing amongst the clouds.

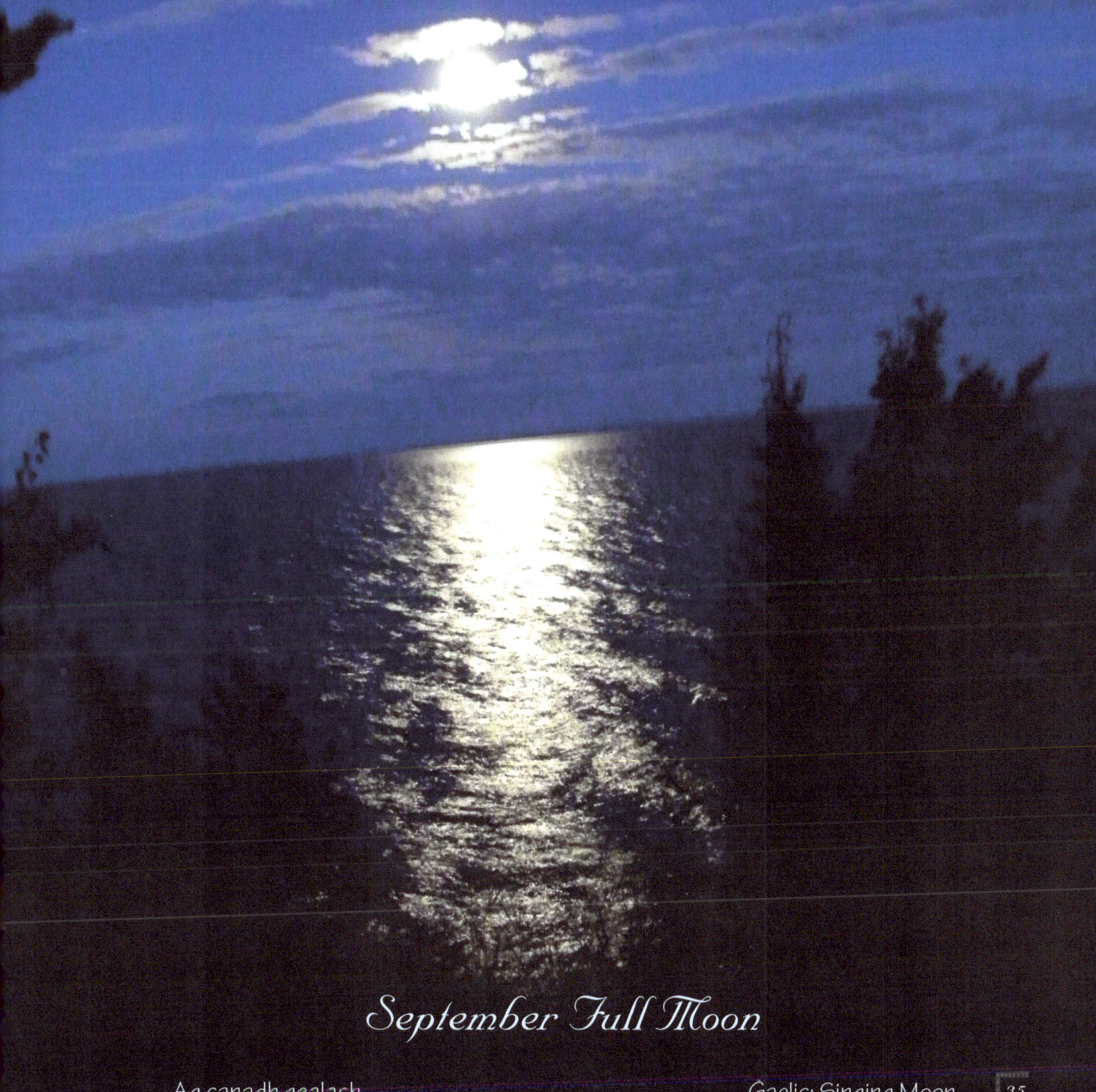

September Full Moon

Ag canadh gealach

Gaelic: Singing Moon

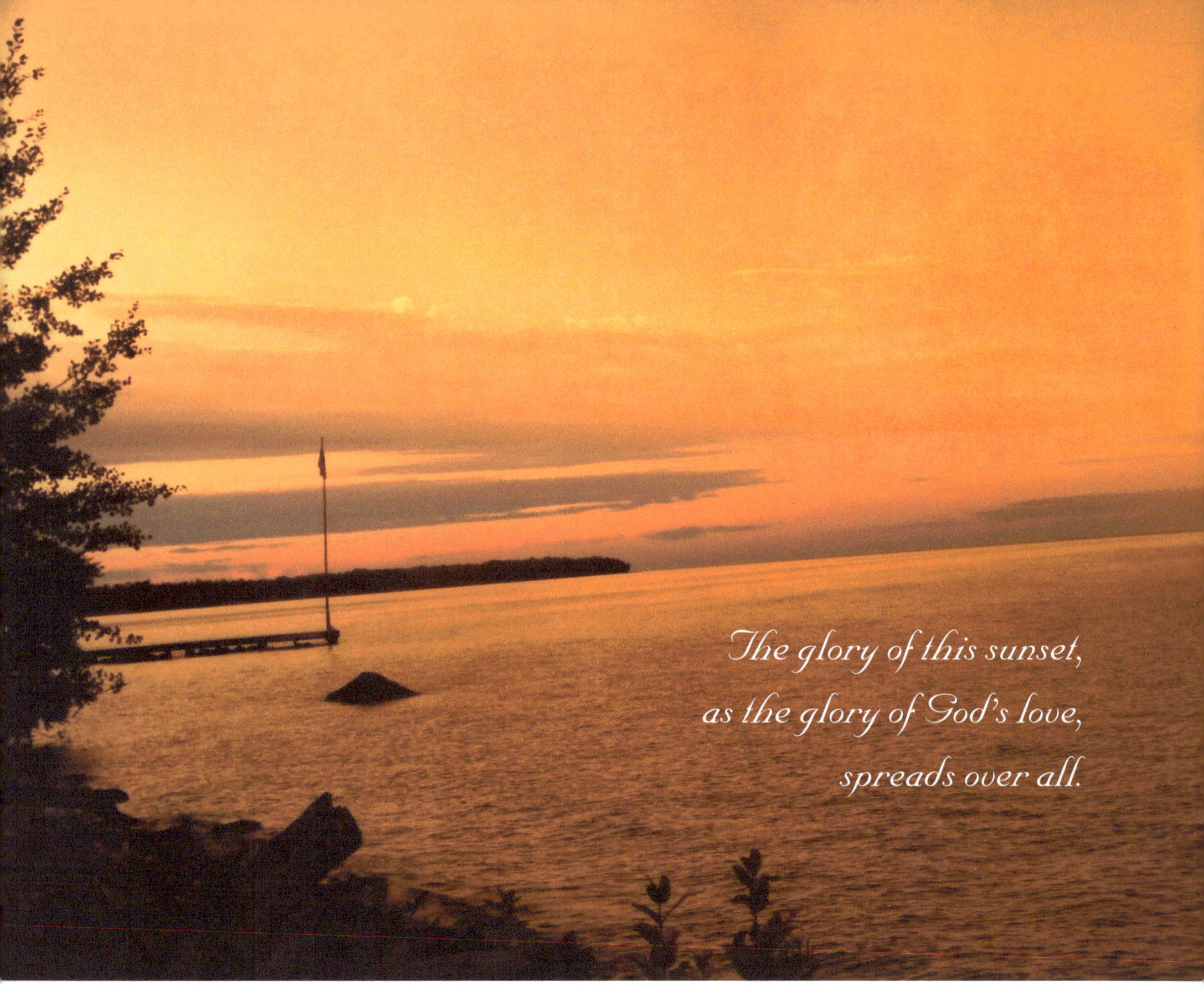

This particular sunset was so dramatic the colors ranged over the entire dome of the sky from west even unto the east, which is the direction this was taken.

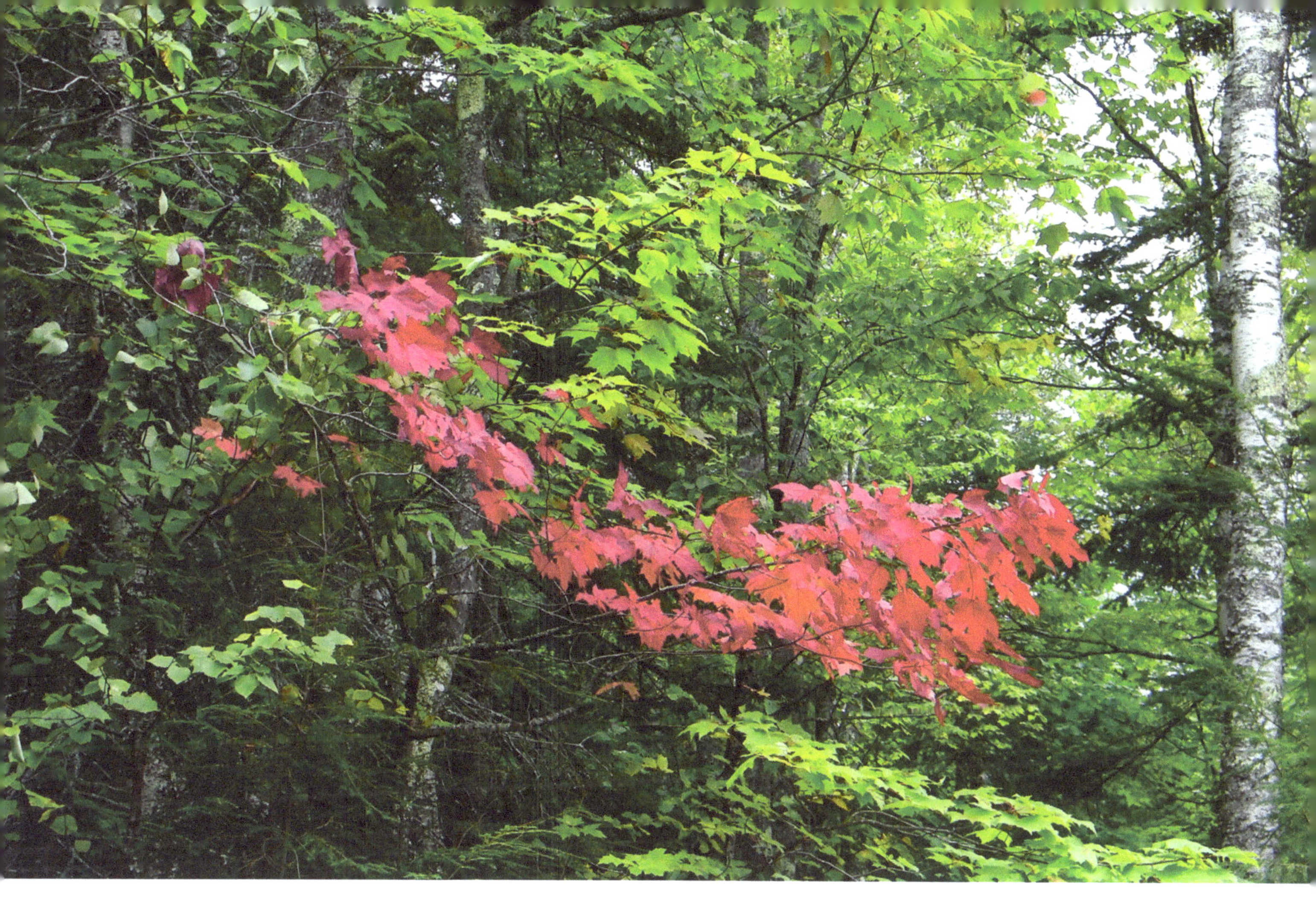

A bright prelim for God's painting to come.

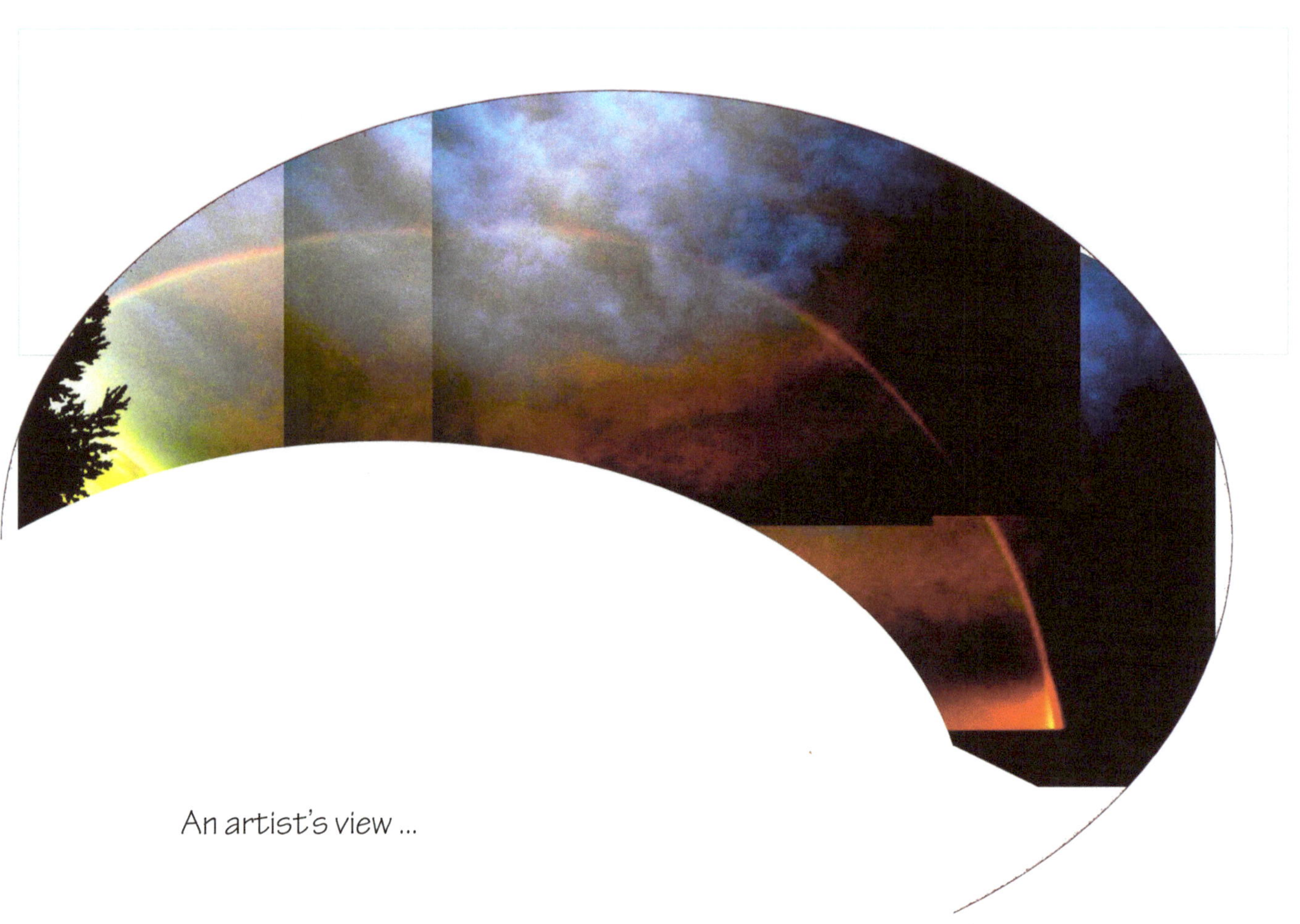

An artist's view ...

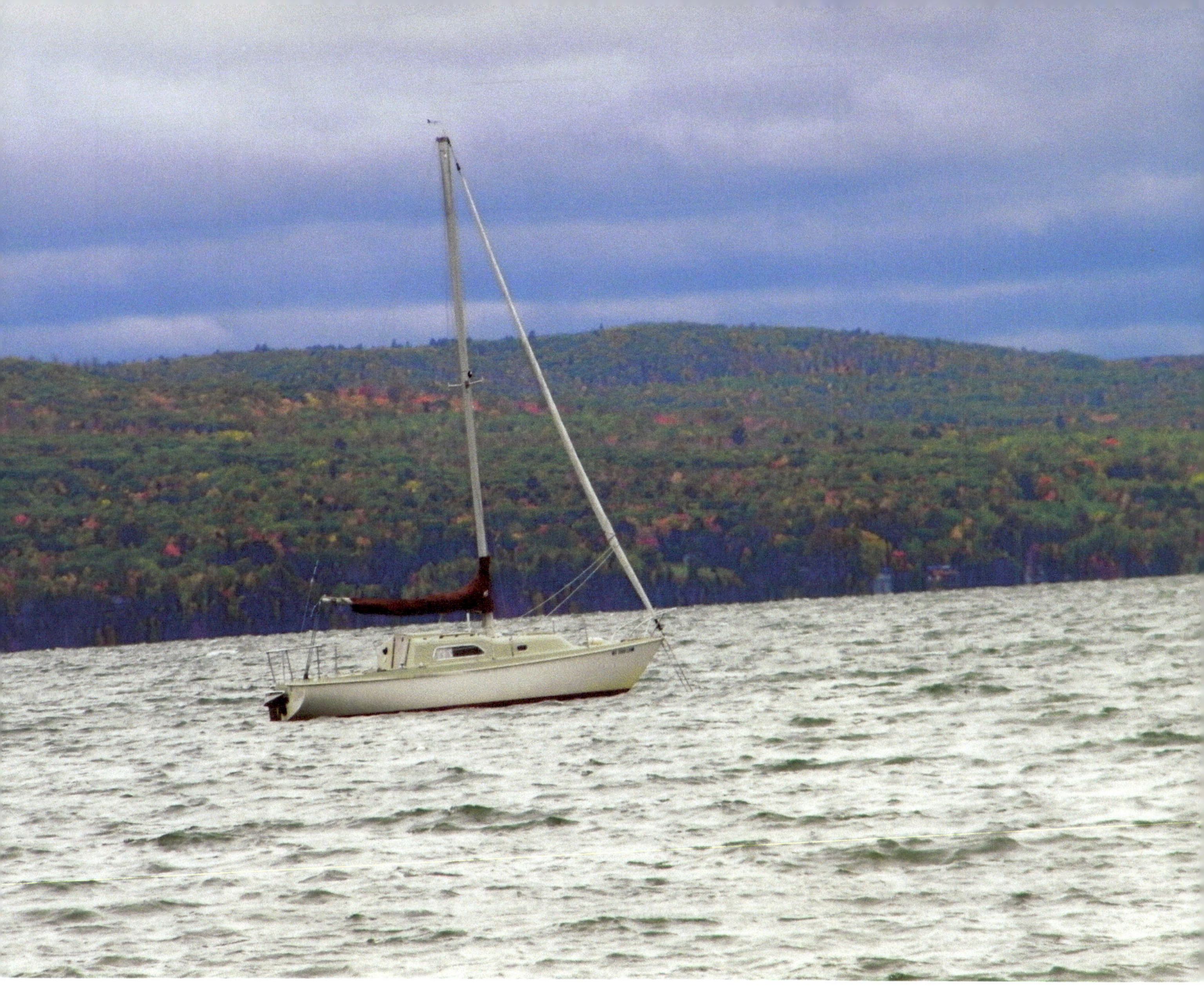

How long can I wait?

As the gold of the maple surrounds the oak,

so God's Love surrounds us so we can grow straight and tall.

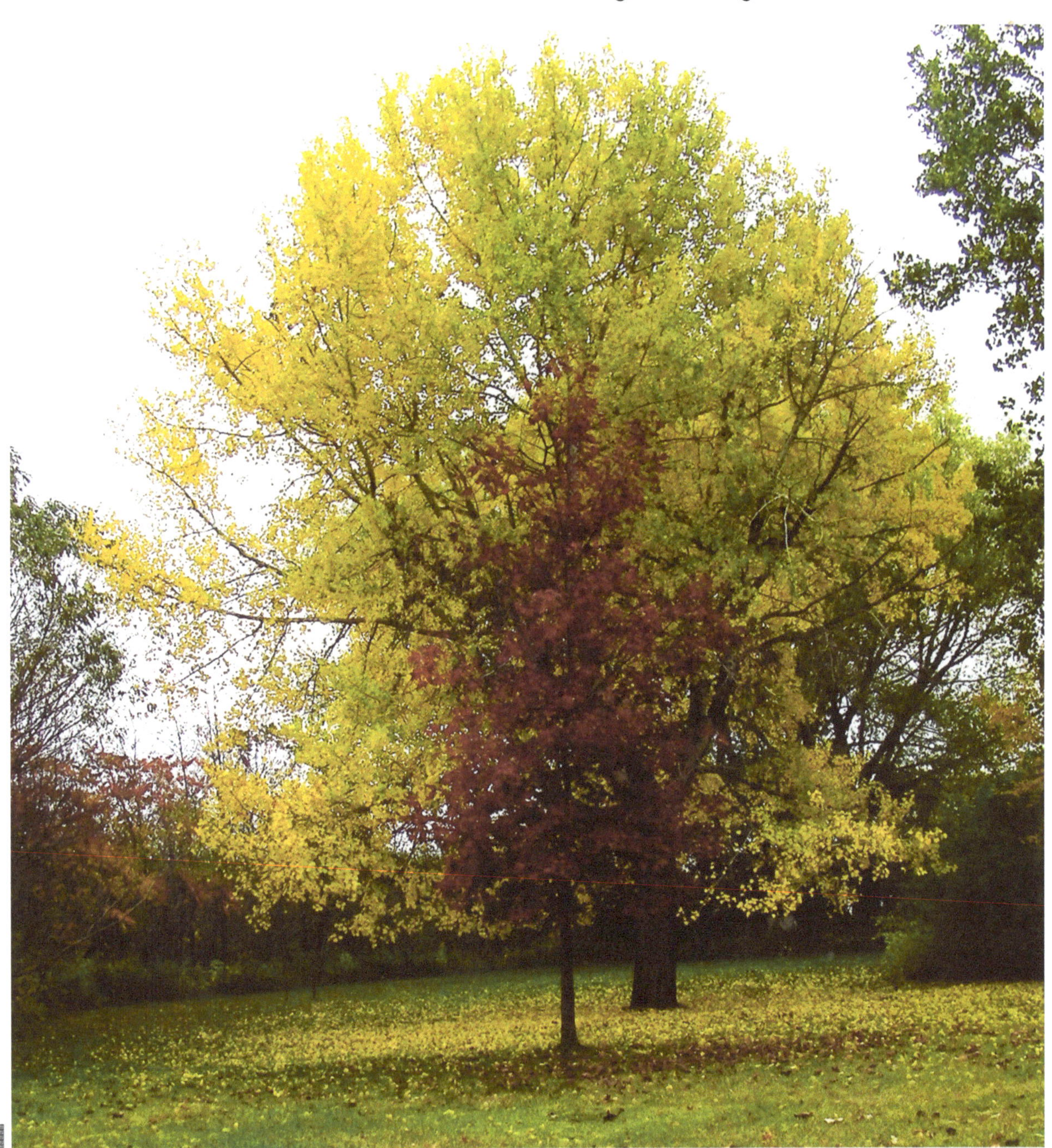

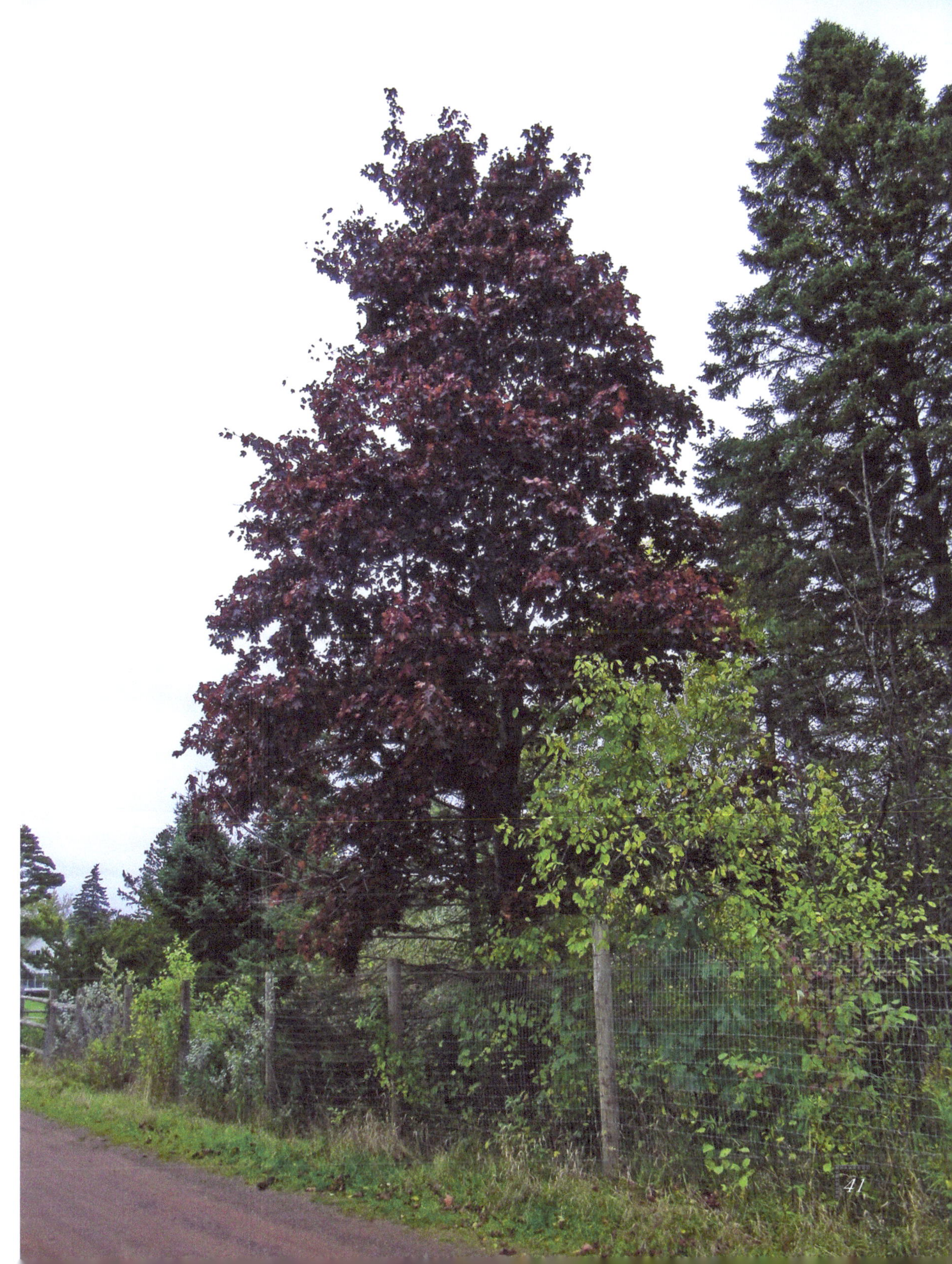

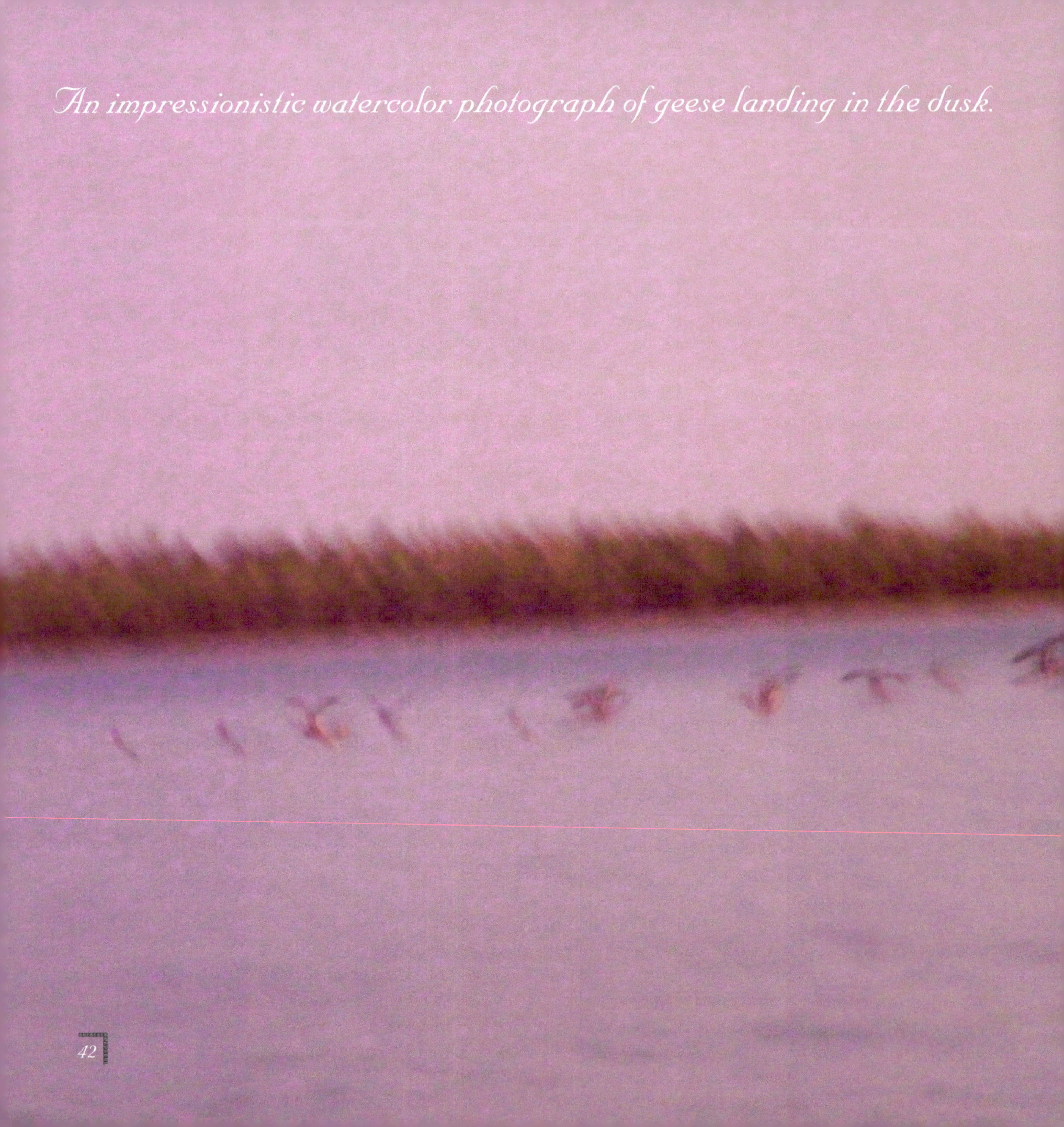

An impressionistic watercolor photograph of geese landing in the dusk.

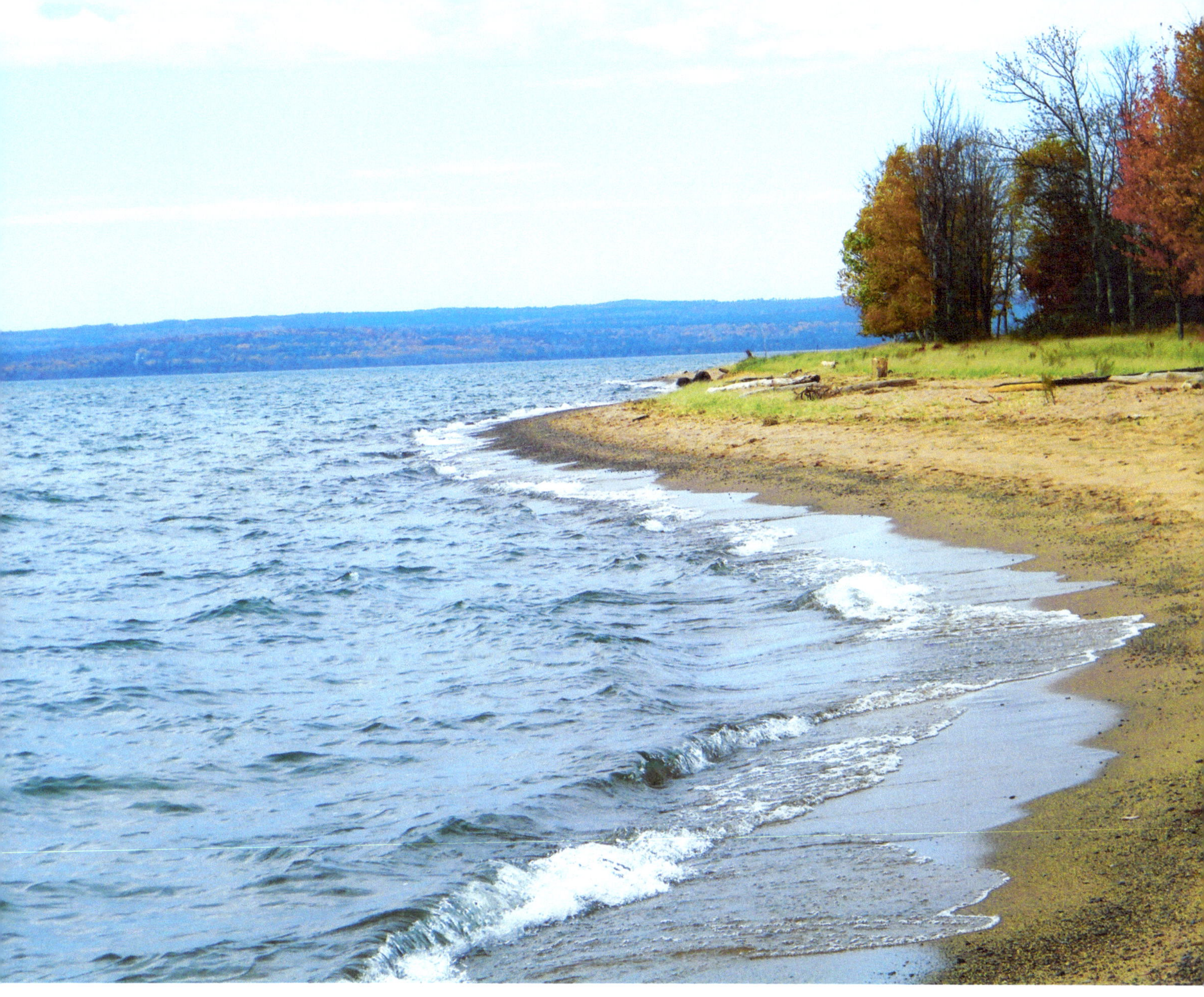

Grant's Point

Where the Ojibwa Spirits met the Island Spirits

and they found a home.

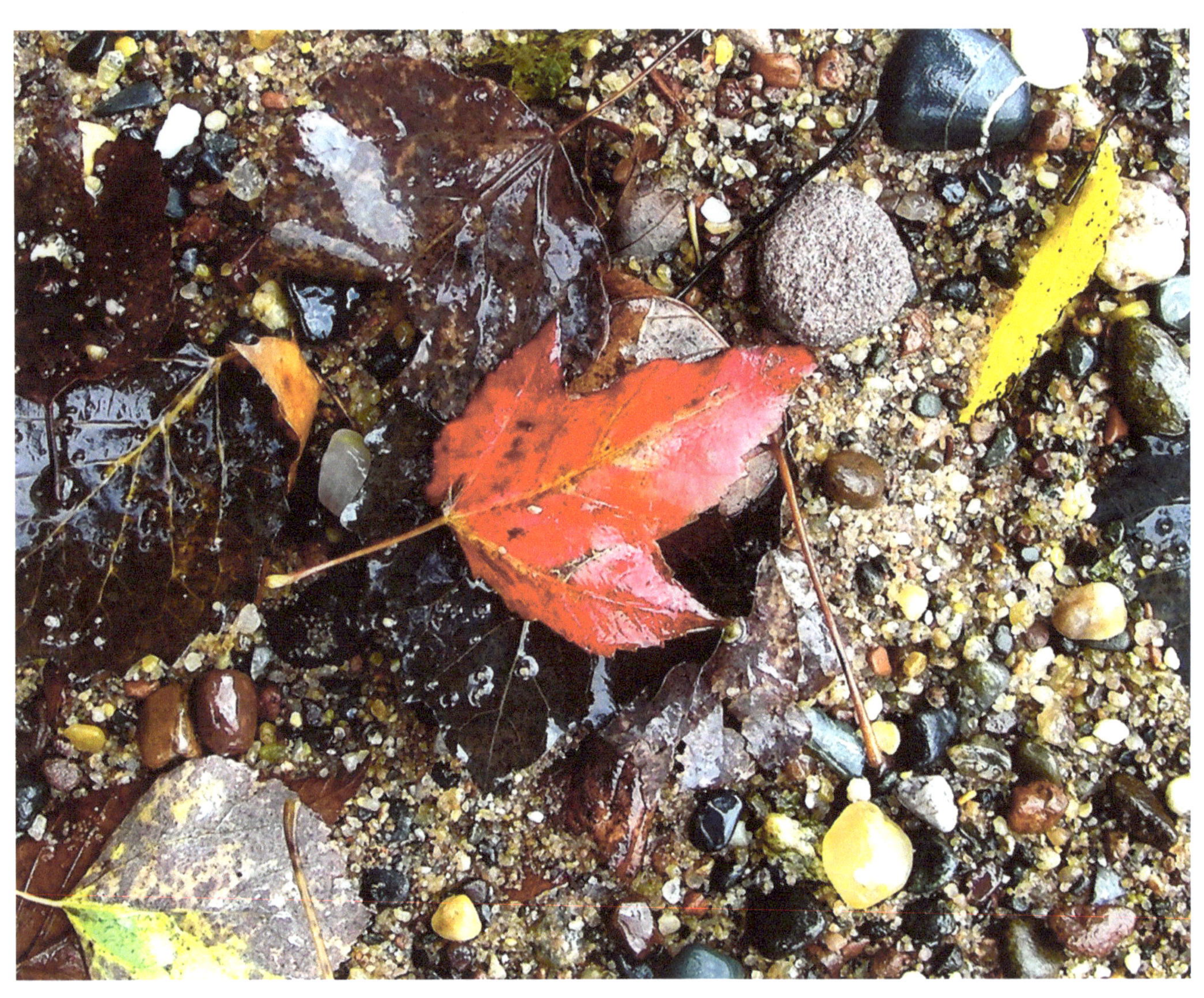

A bright bit of color.

Where the Island keeps

her golden treasure.

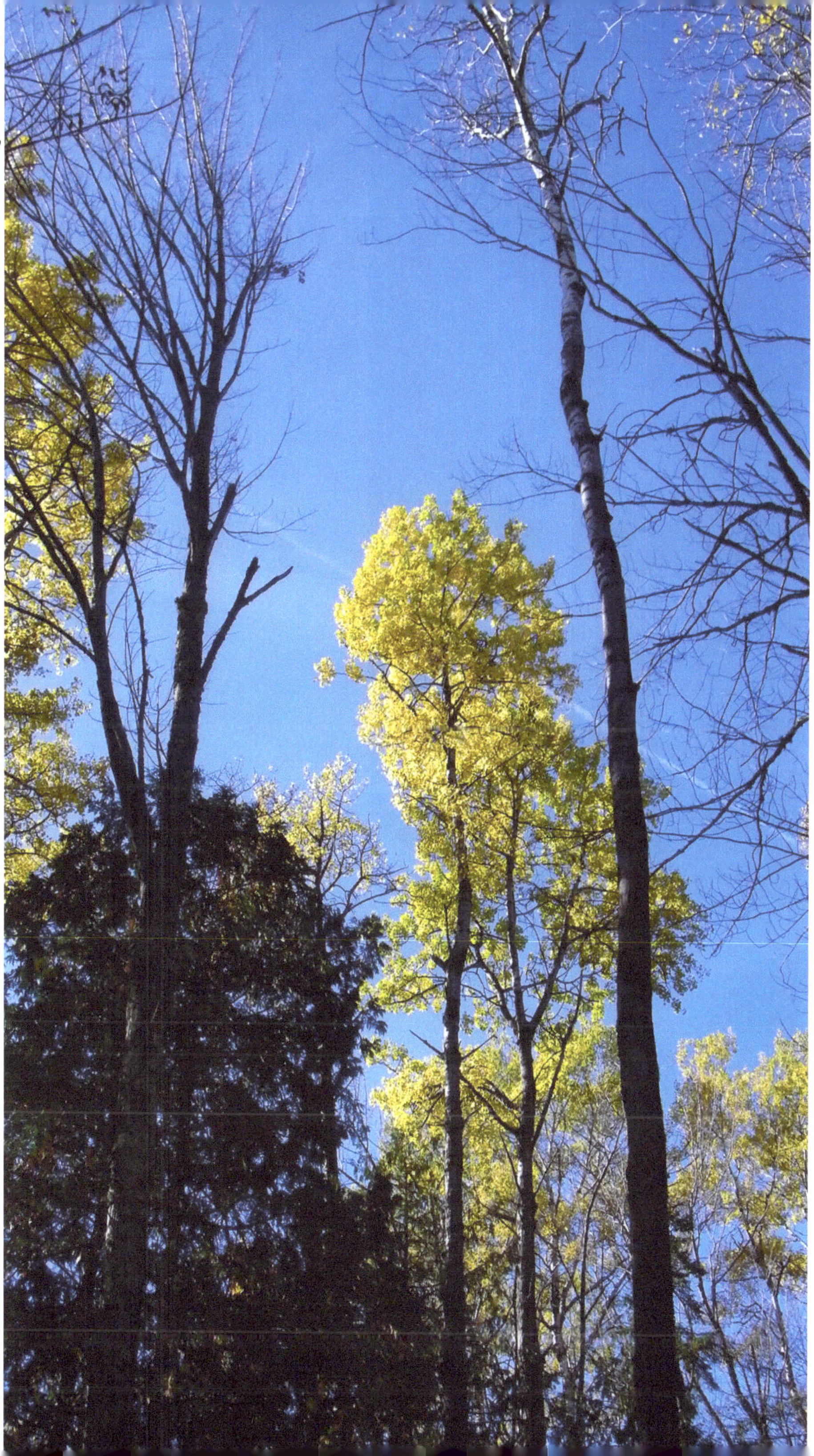

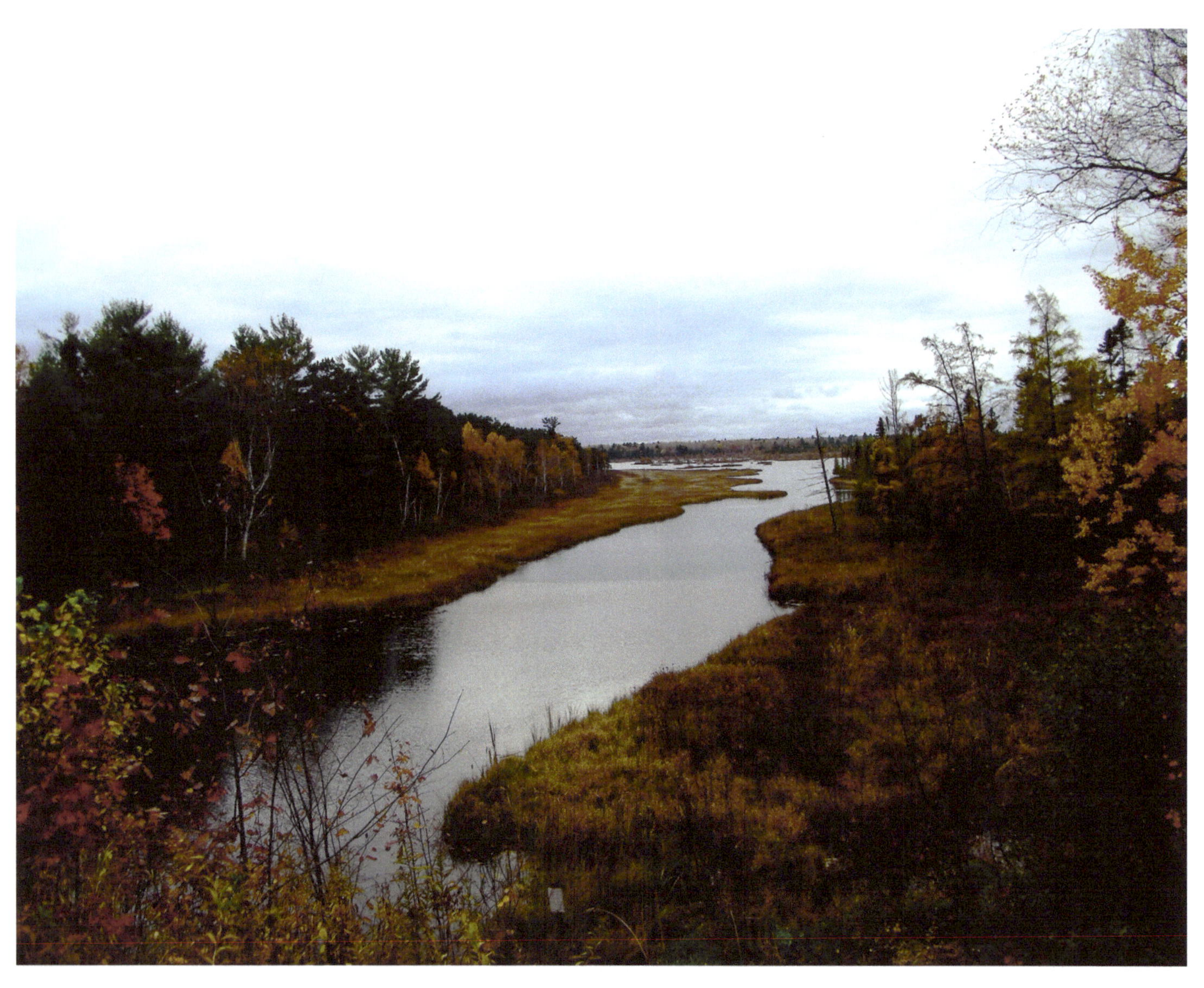

Autumn settles on the lagoon.

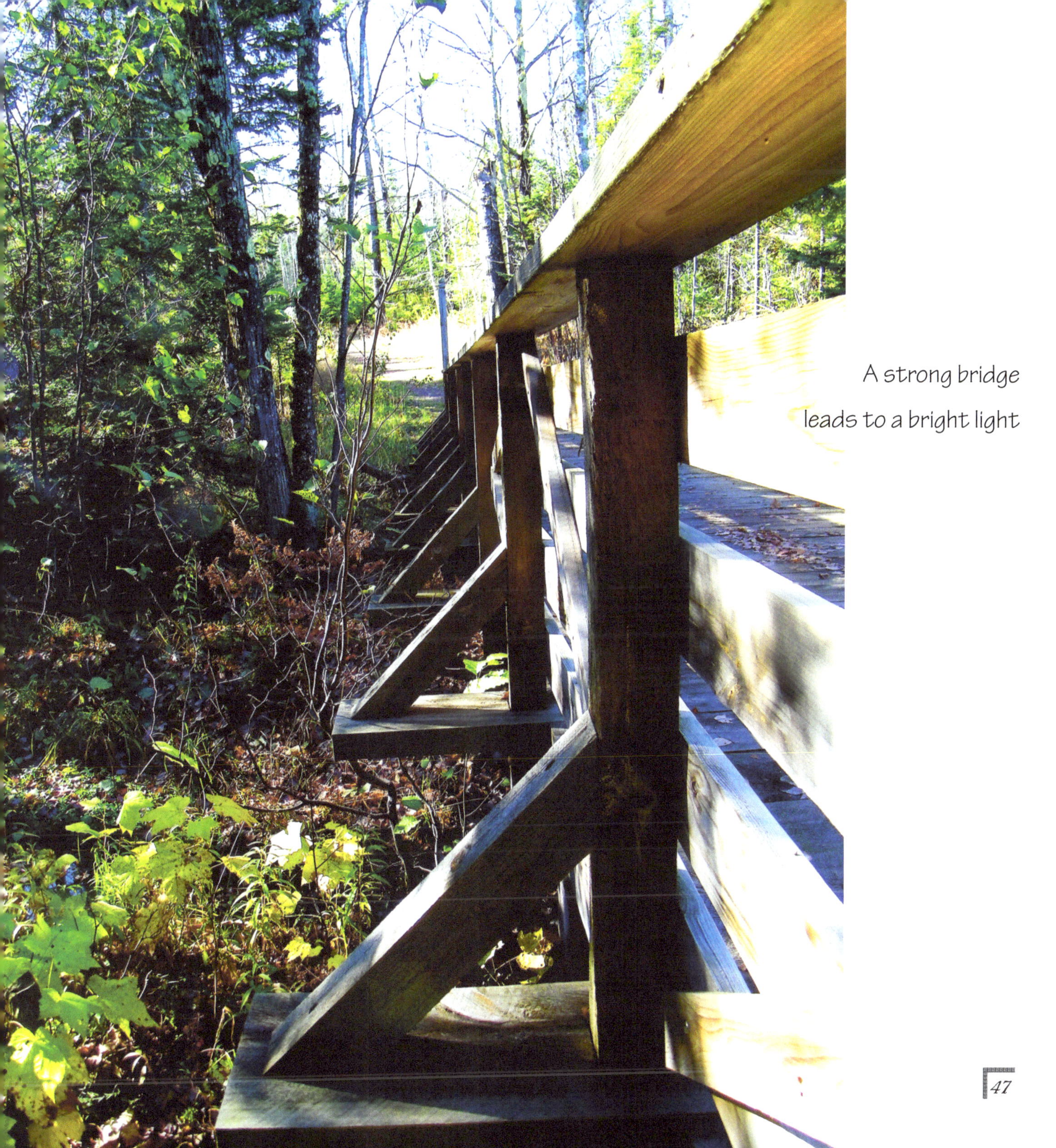

A strong bridge
leads to a bright light

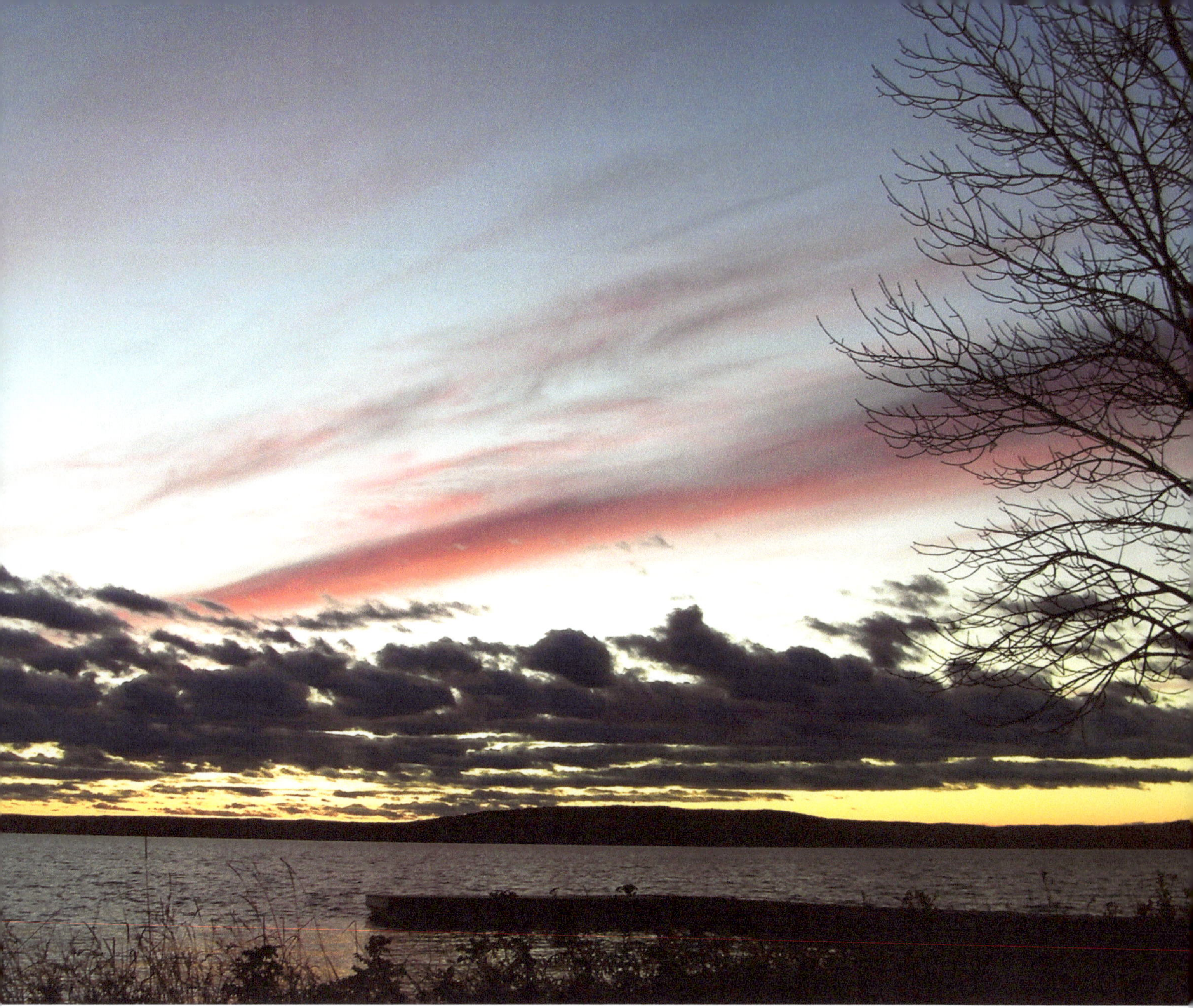

Sunset from Joni's beach. I thought the sun was gone and I had missed the sunset display. But even though it was over the horizon, even though it appeared to disappear, it continued to blaze us with a brilliantly painted sky.

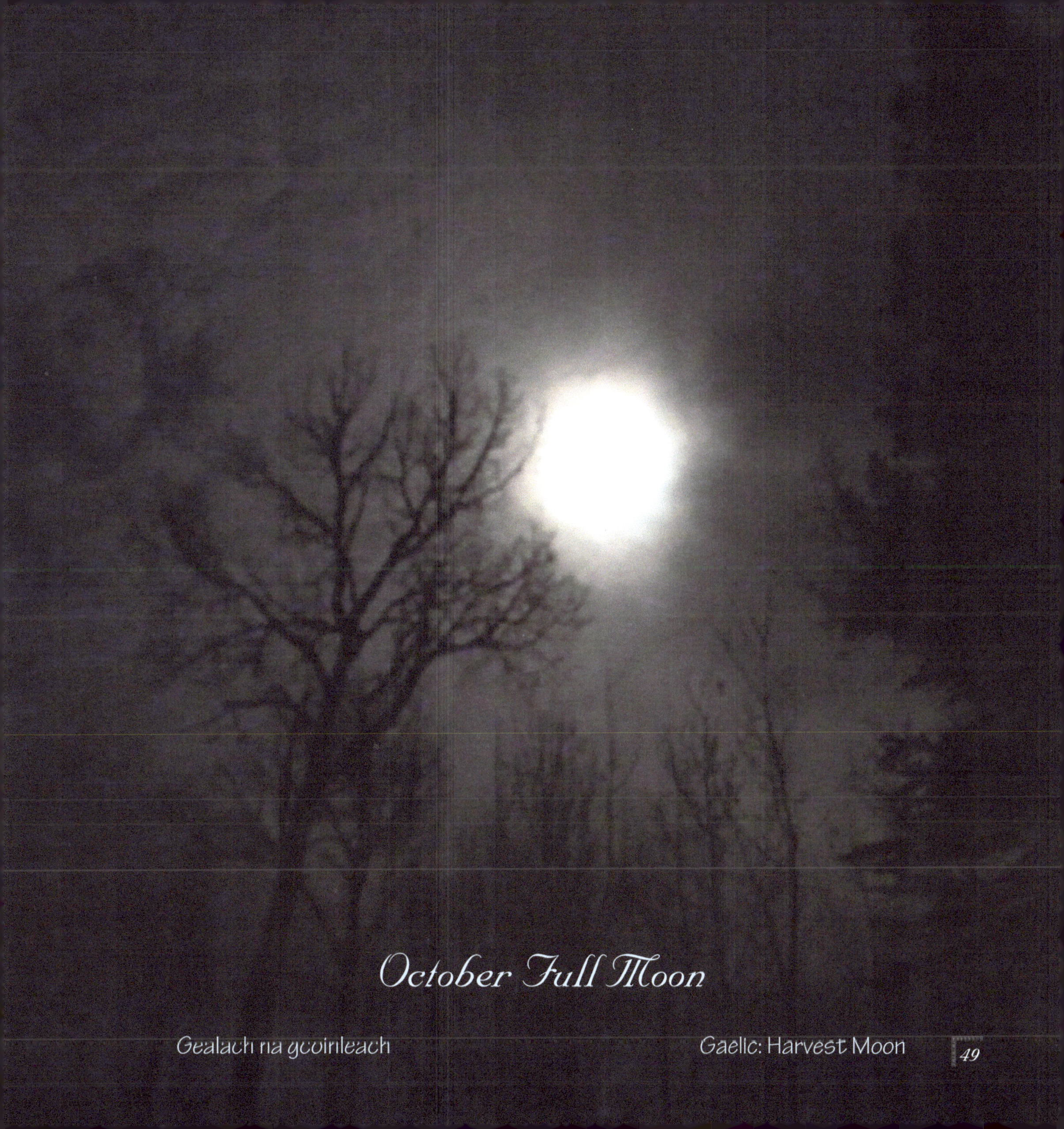

October Full Moon

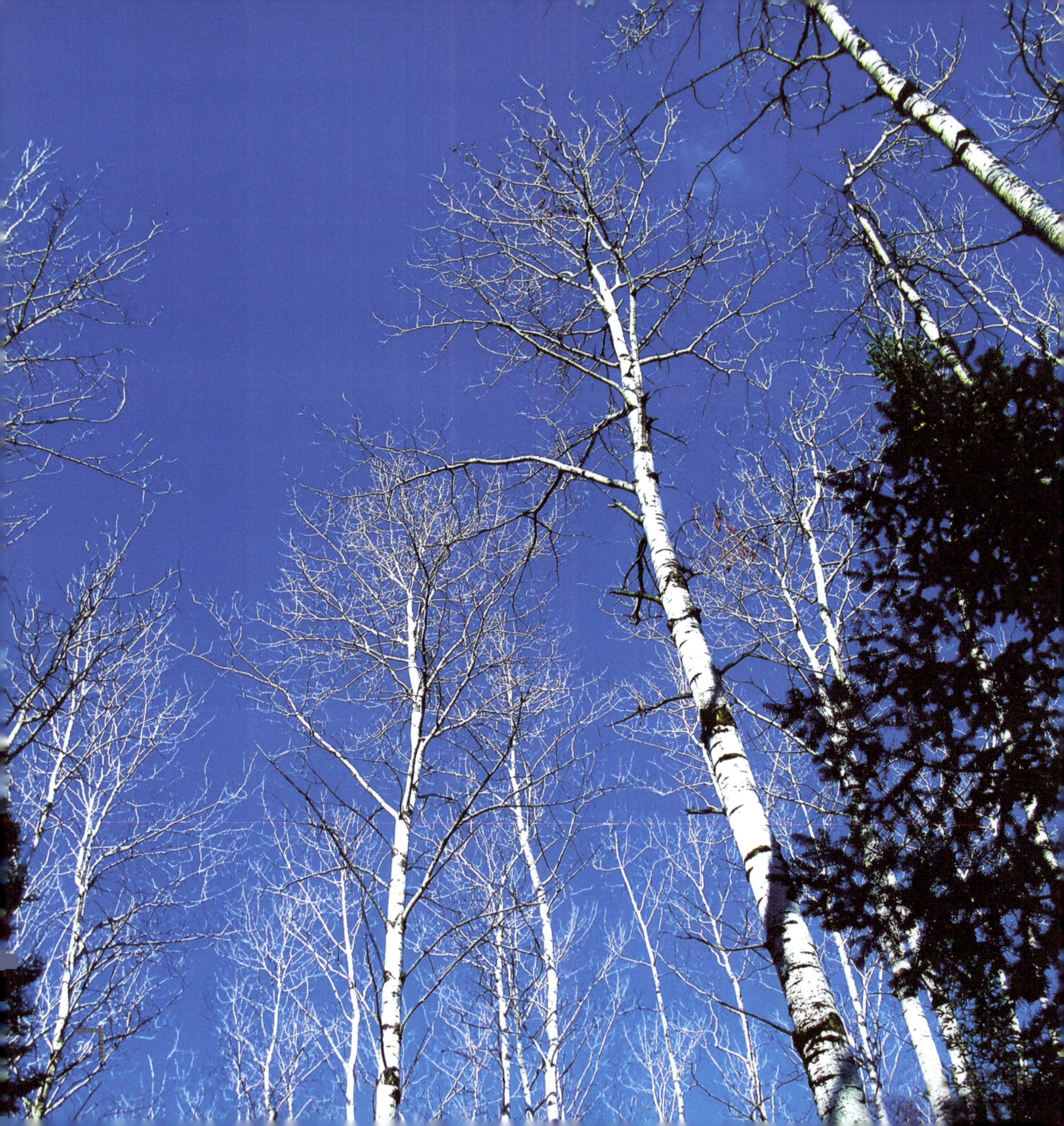

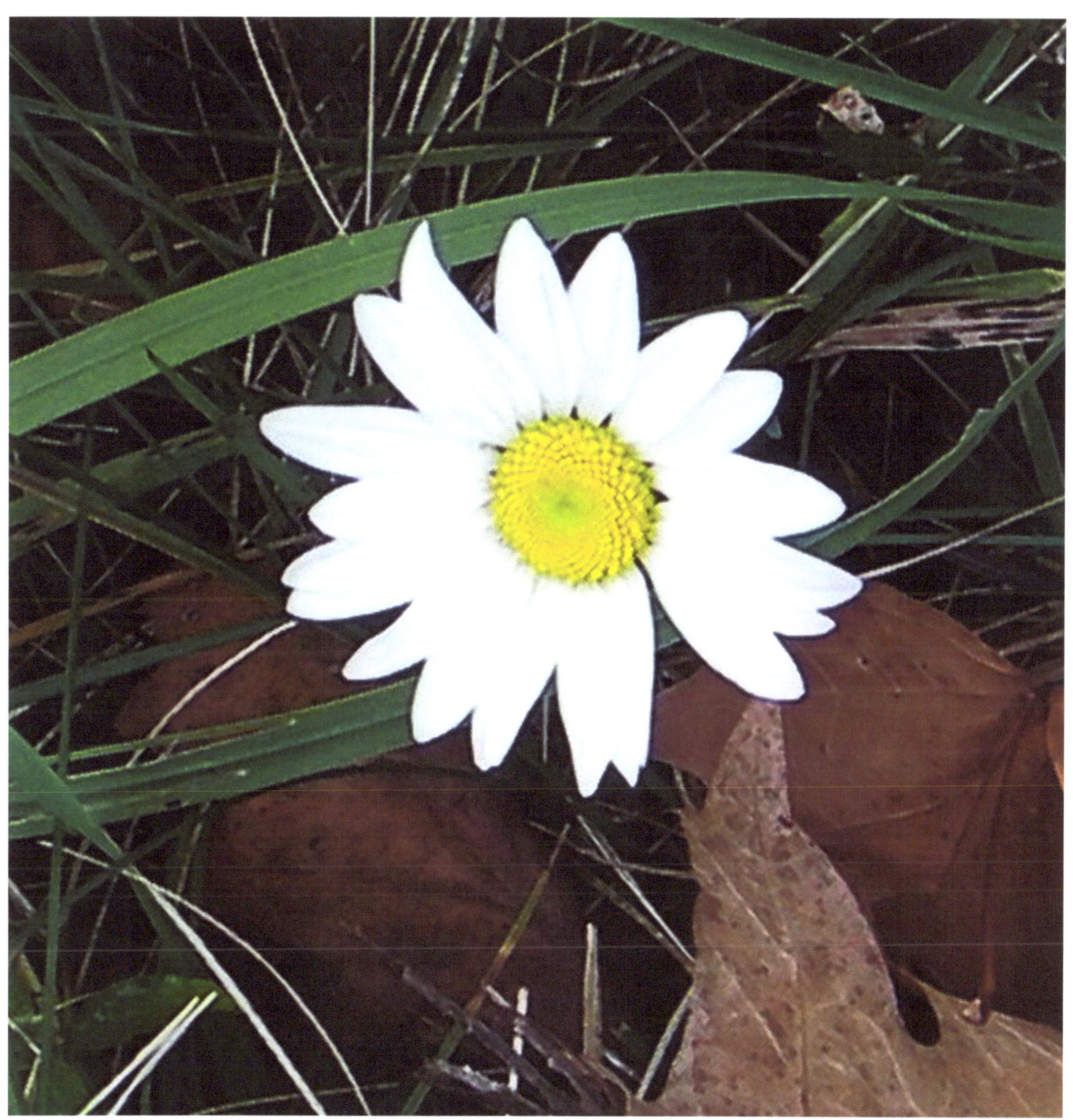

A last spot of summer amidst the autumn grasses.

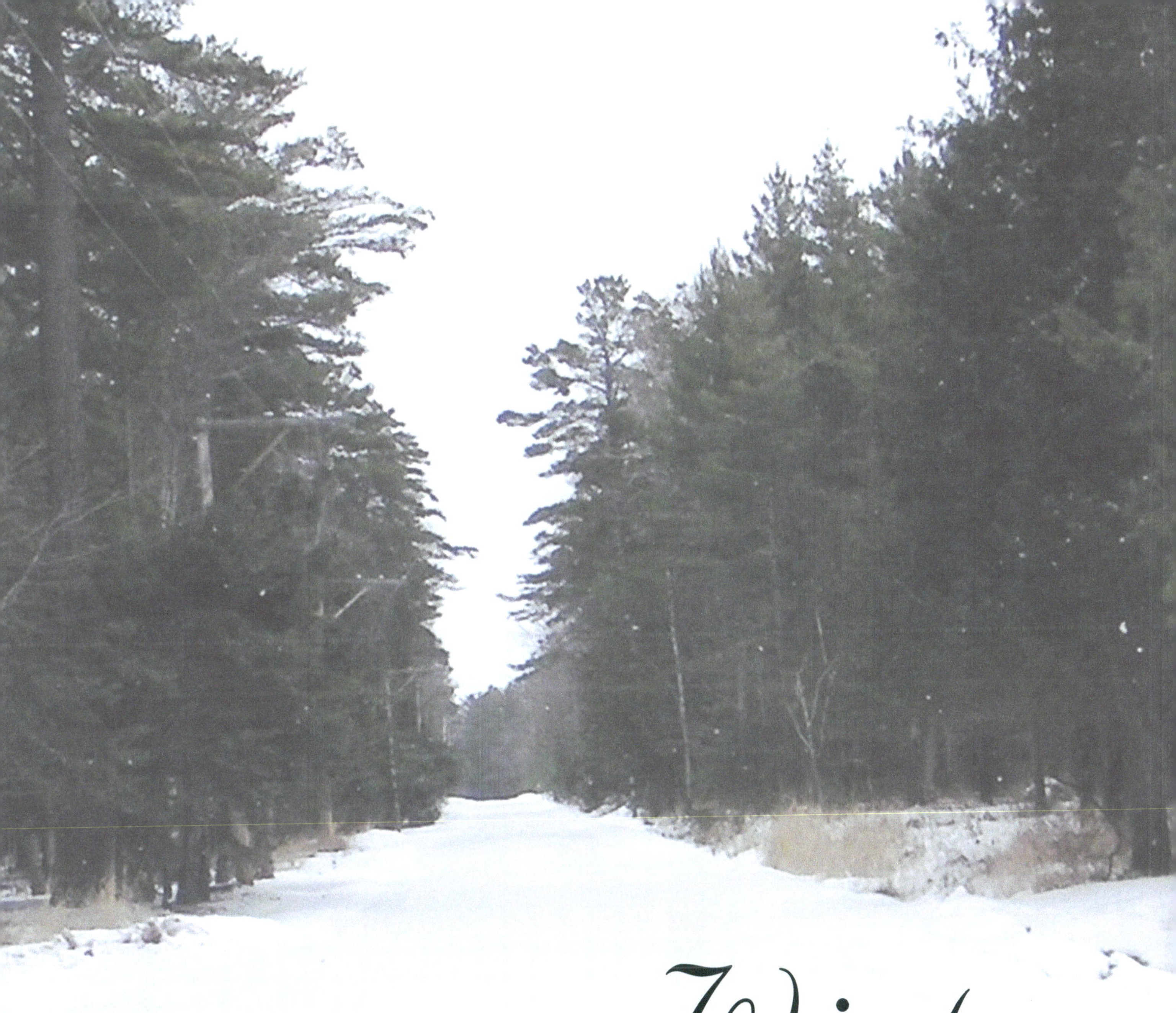
Winter

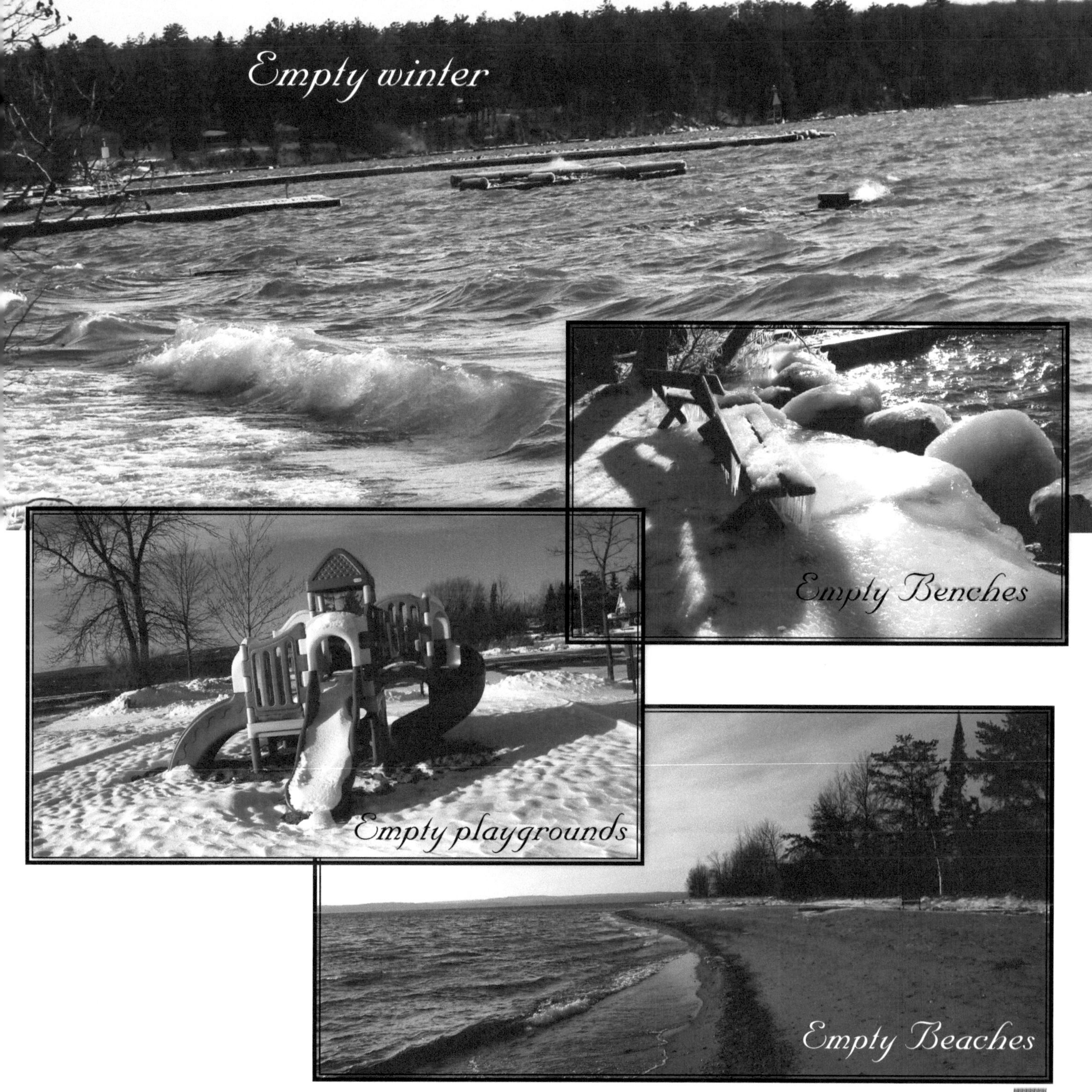

Empty winter
Empty Benches
Empty playgrounds
Empty Beaches

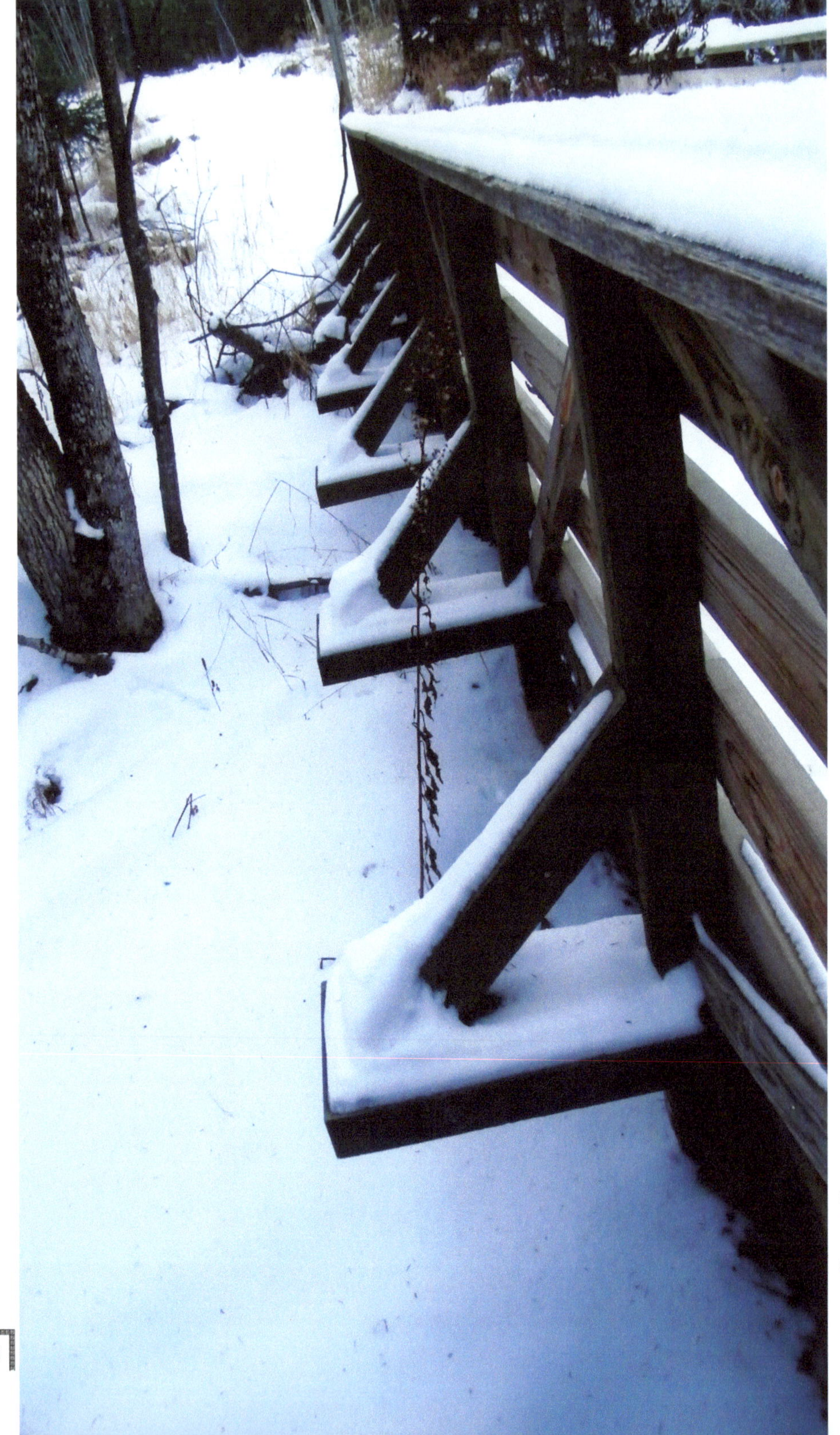

Wherever one can find

strength ...

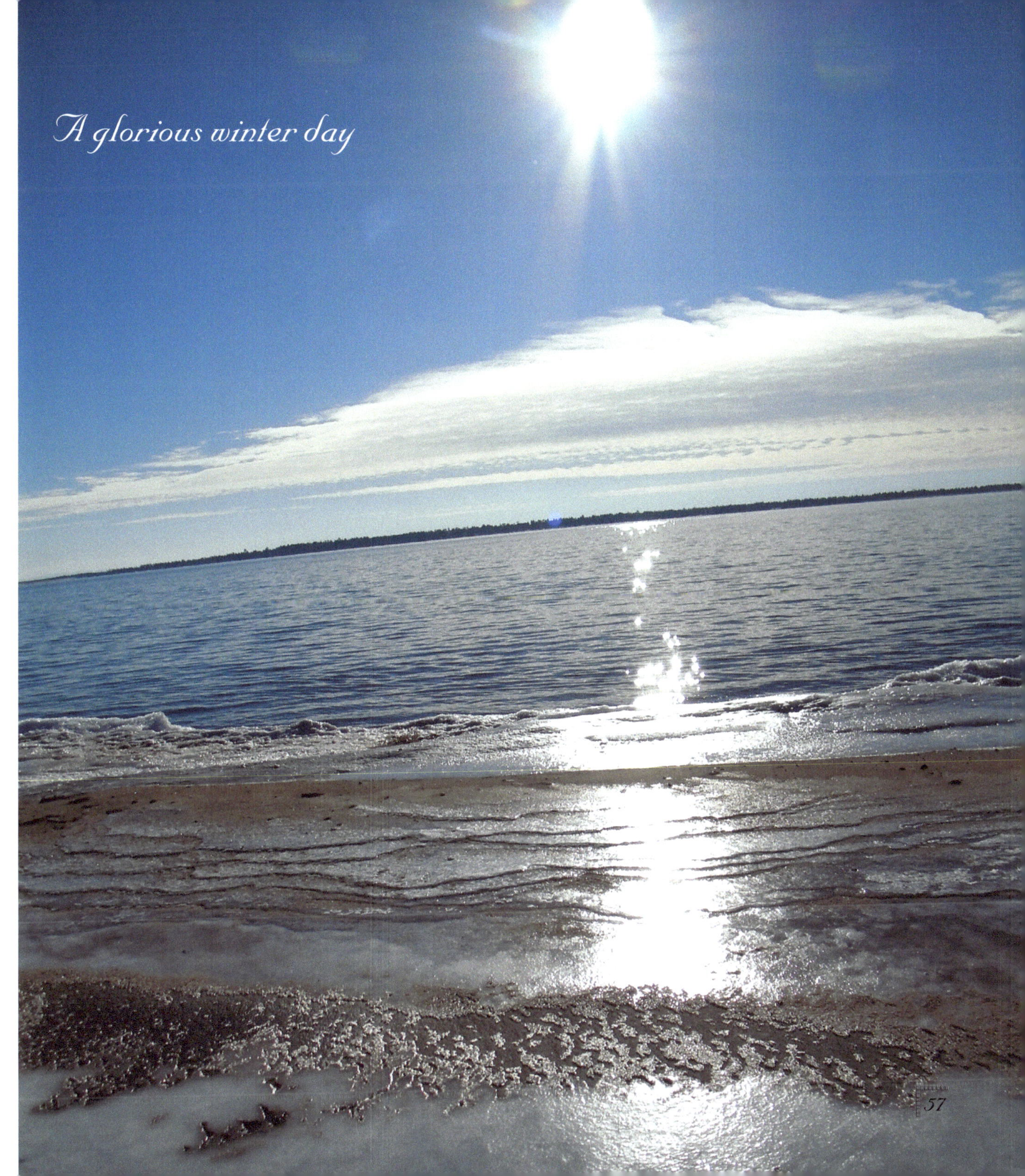
A glorious winter day

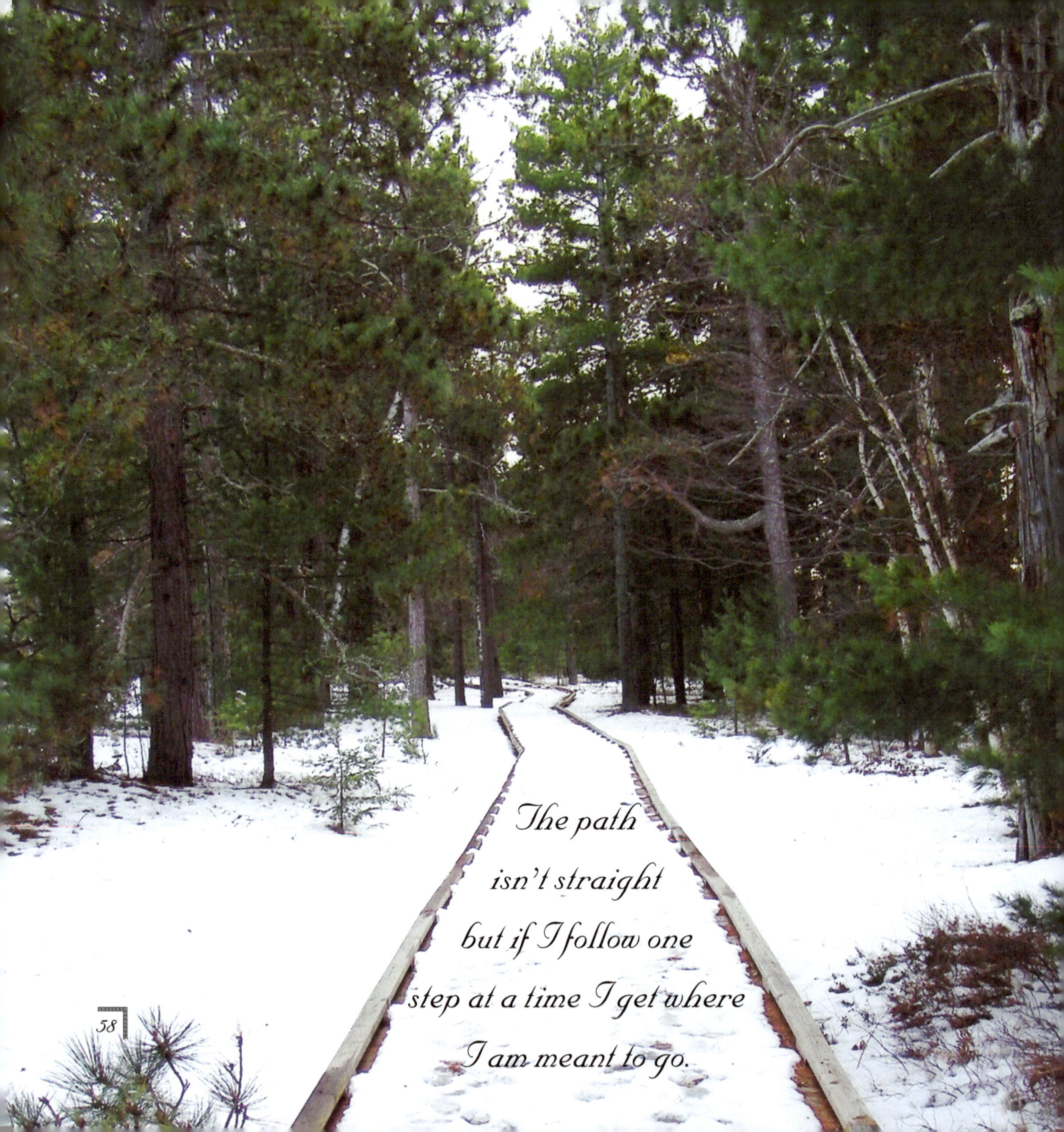

The path
isn't straight
but if I follow one
step at a time I get where
I am meant to go.

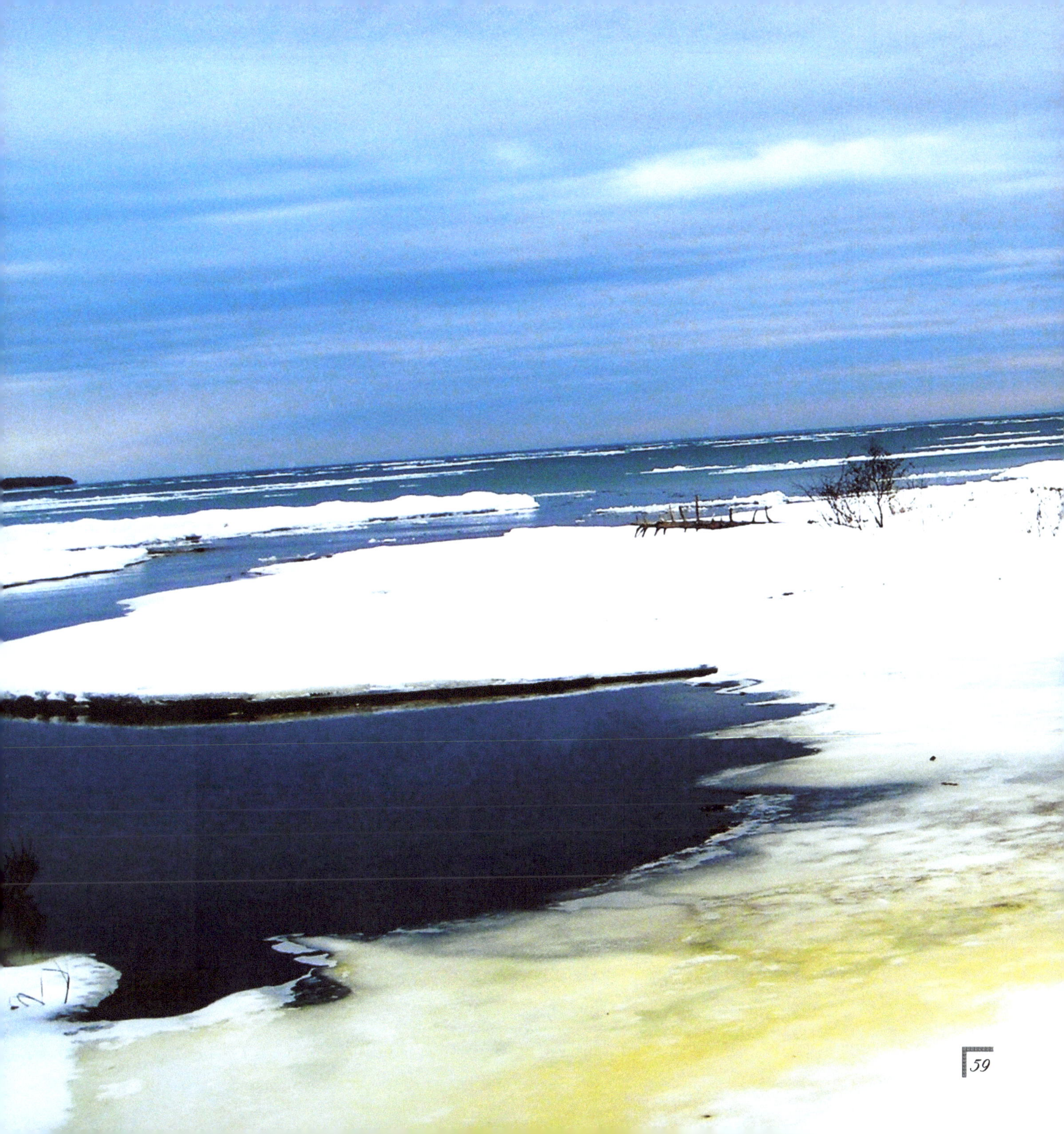

Reflections on the water, like shadows in my mind,

speak to me of passing days and nights and passing times.

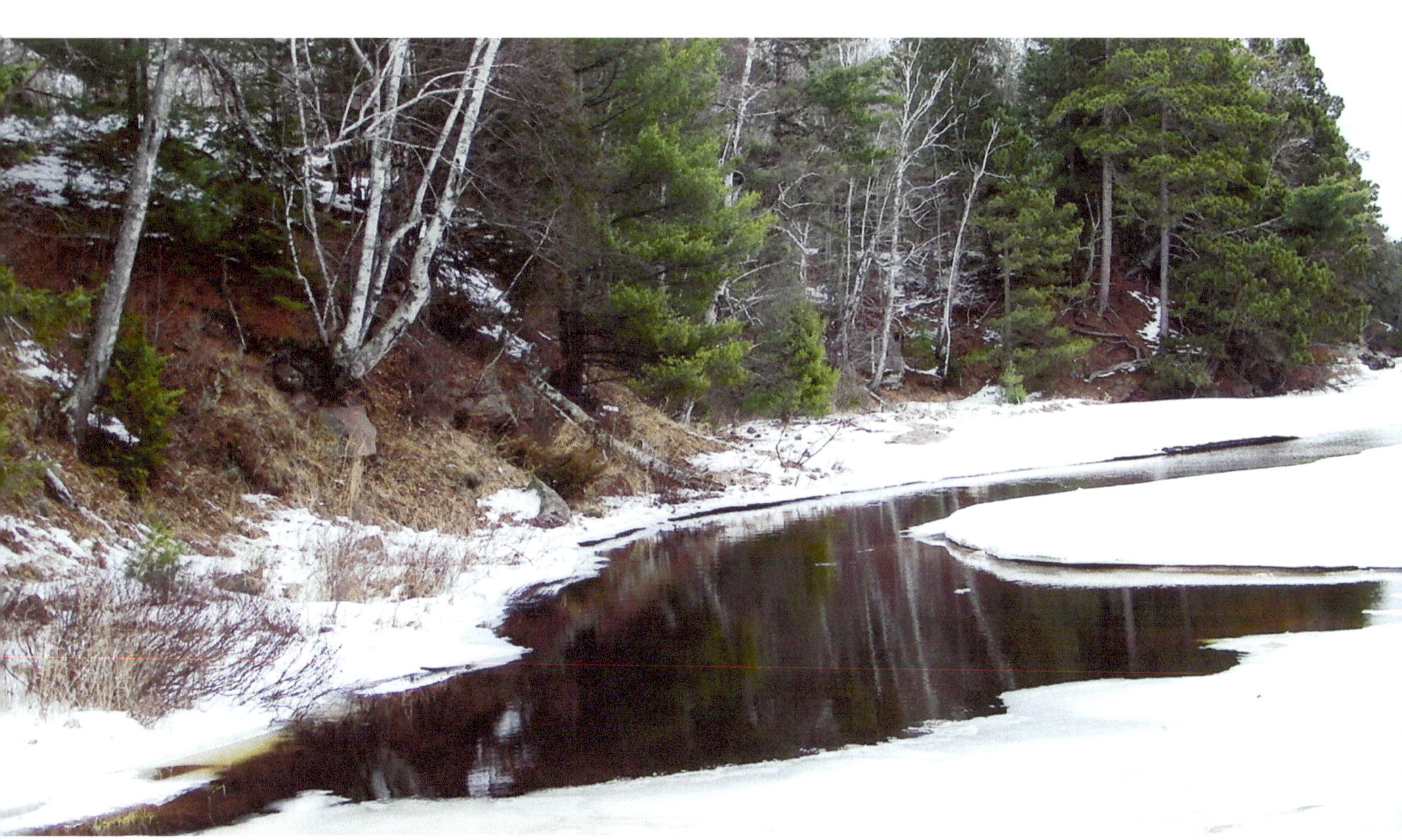

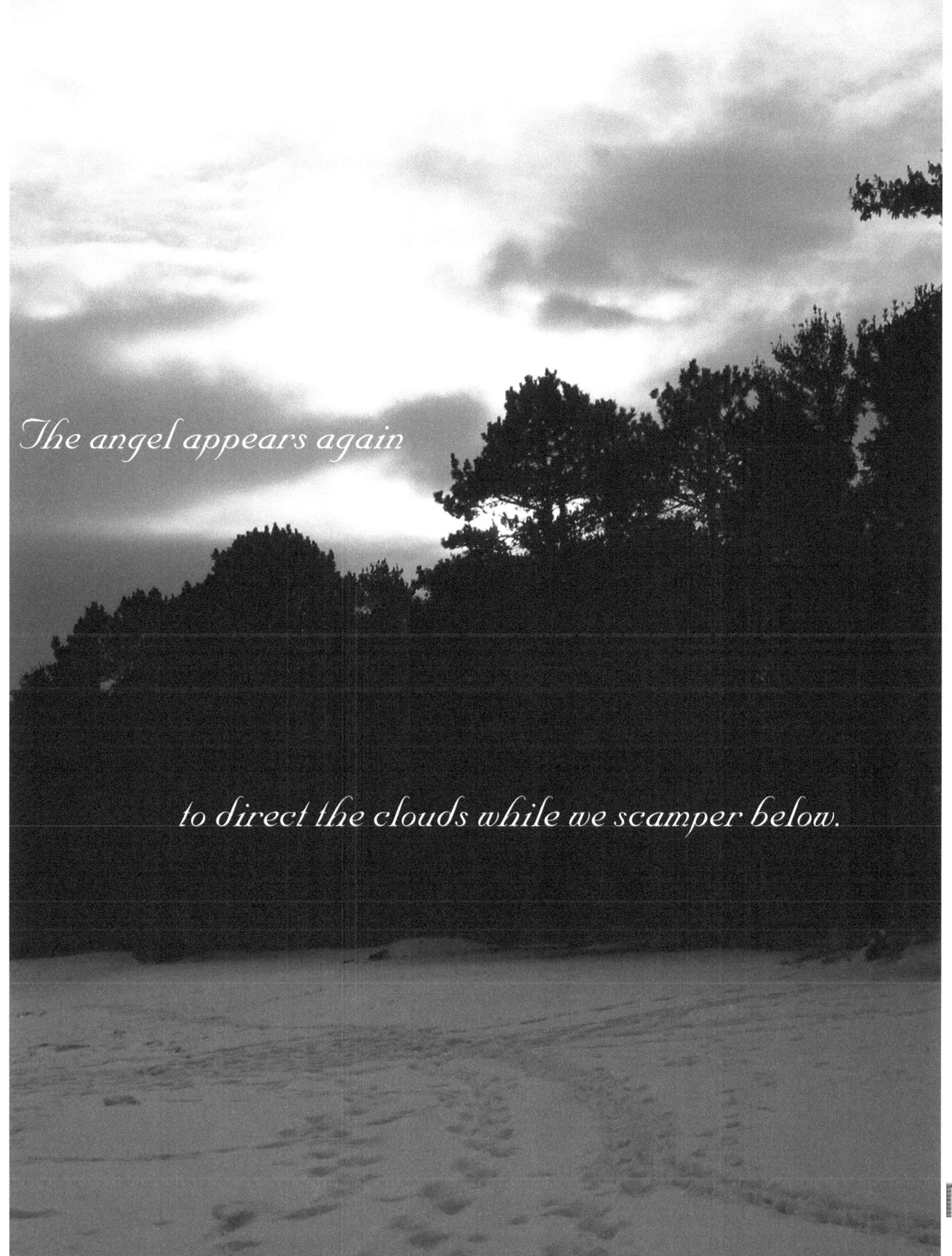

The angel appears again
to direct the clouds while we scamper below.

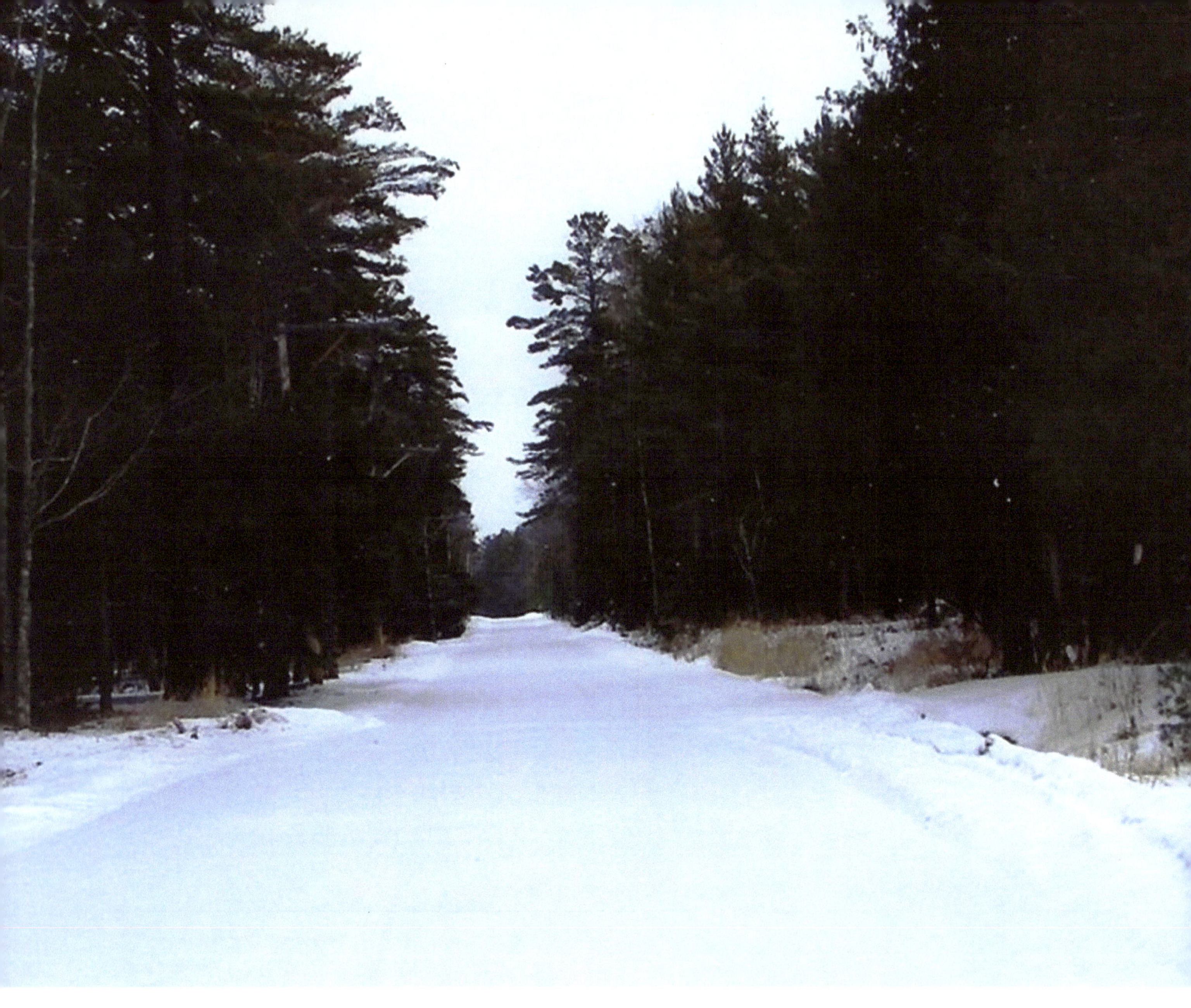

Someone has to be first ...

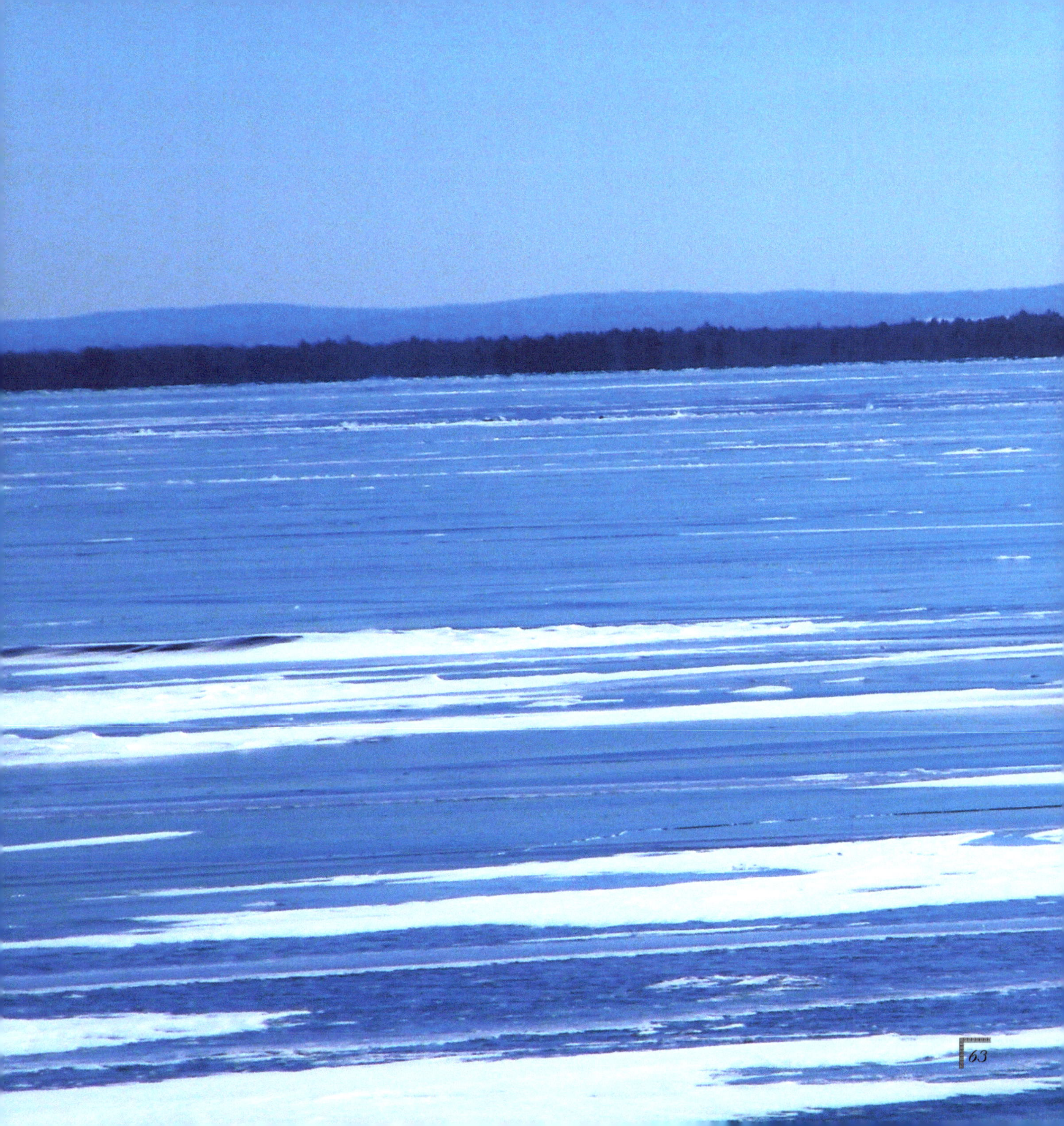

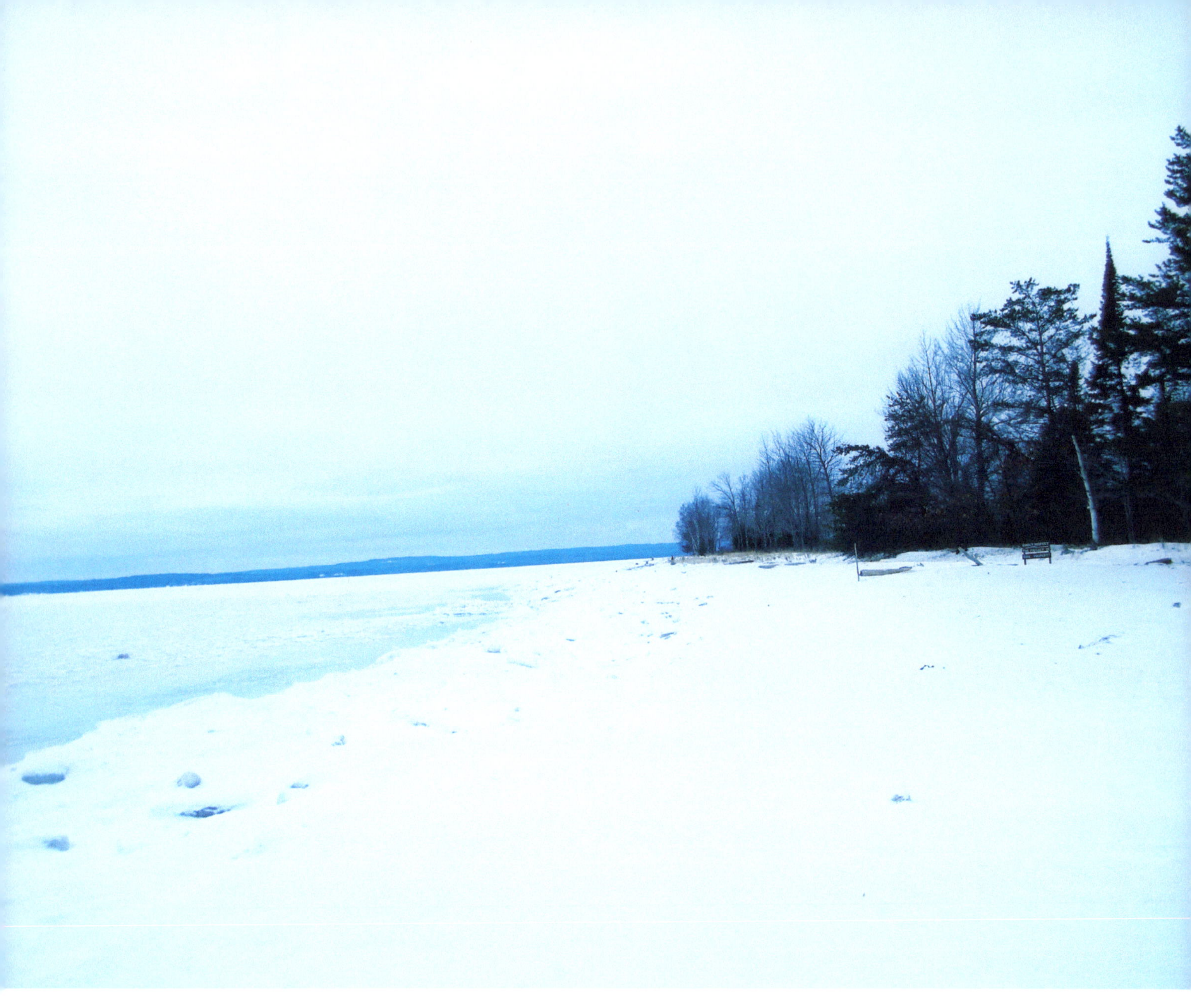

Grant's Point beach buried in ice and snow.

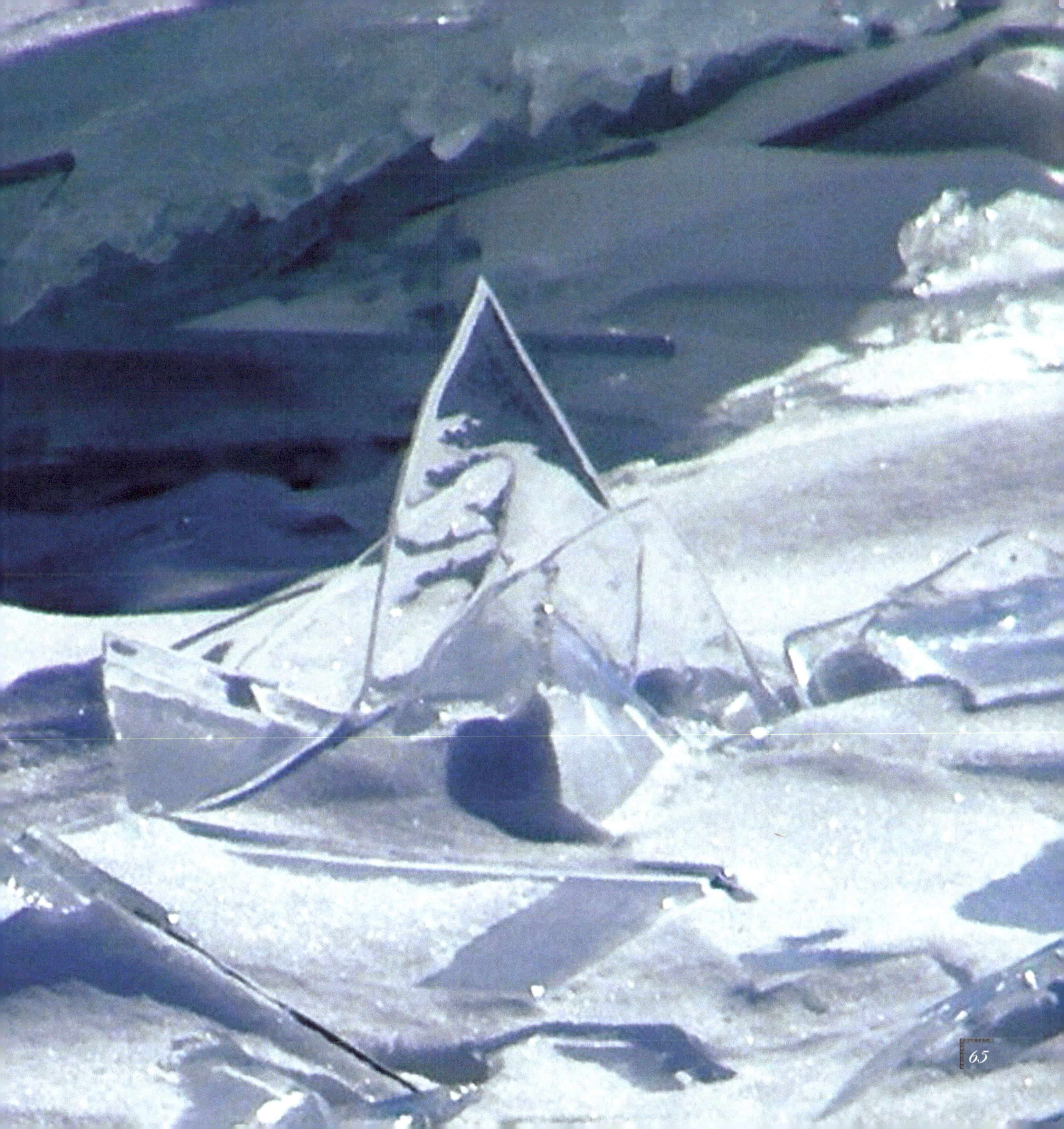

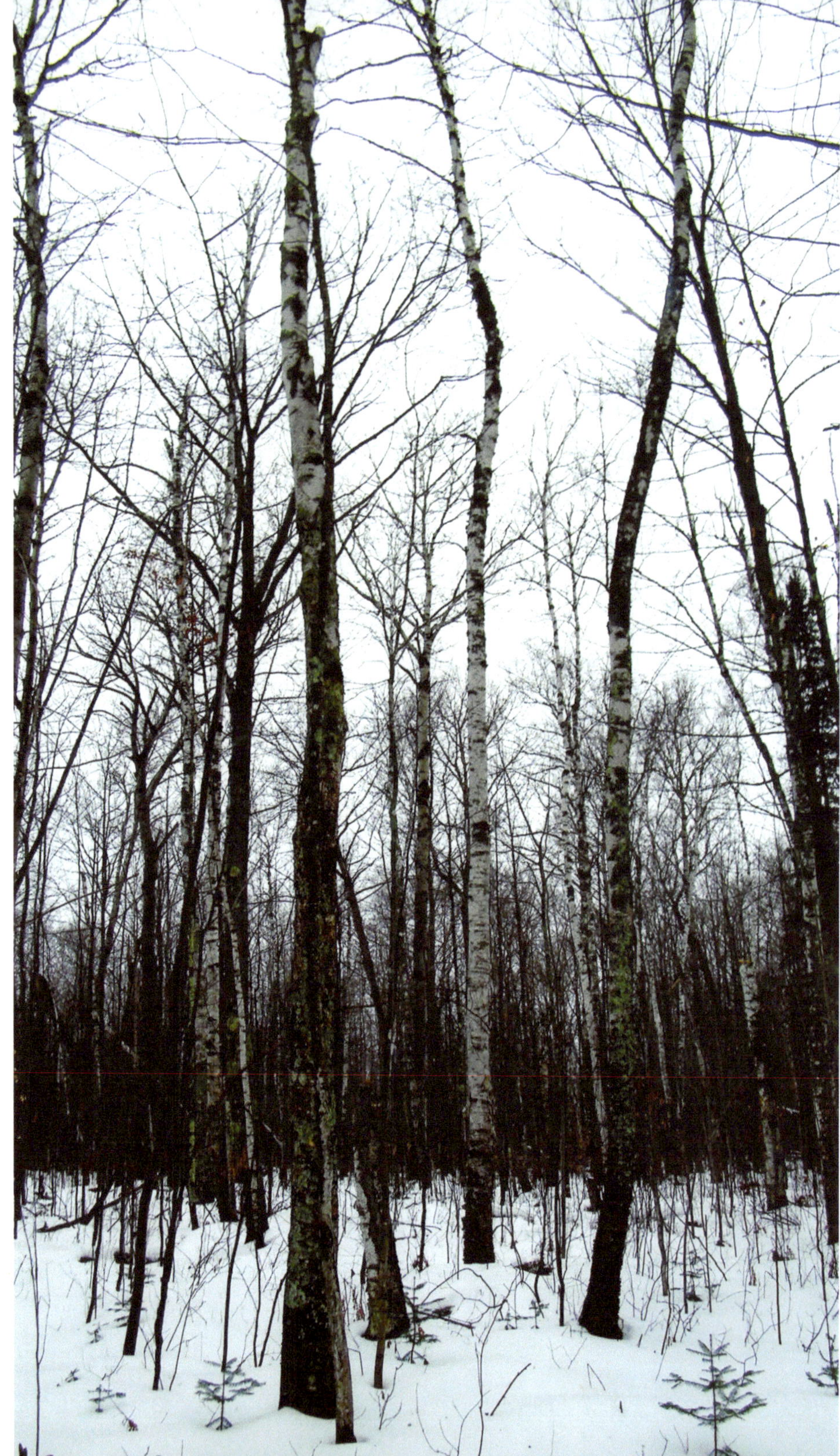

Can you hear the silence?

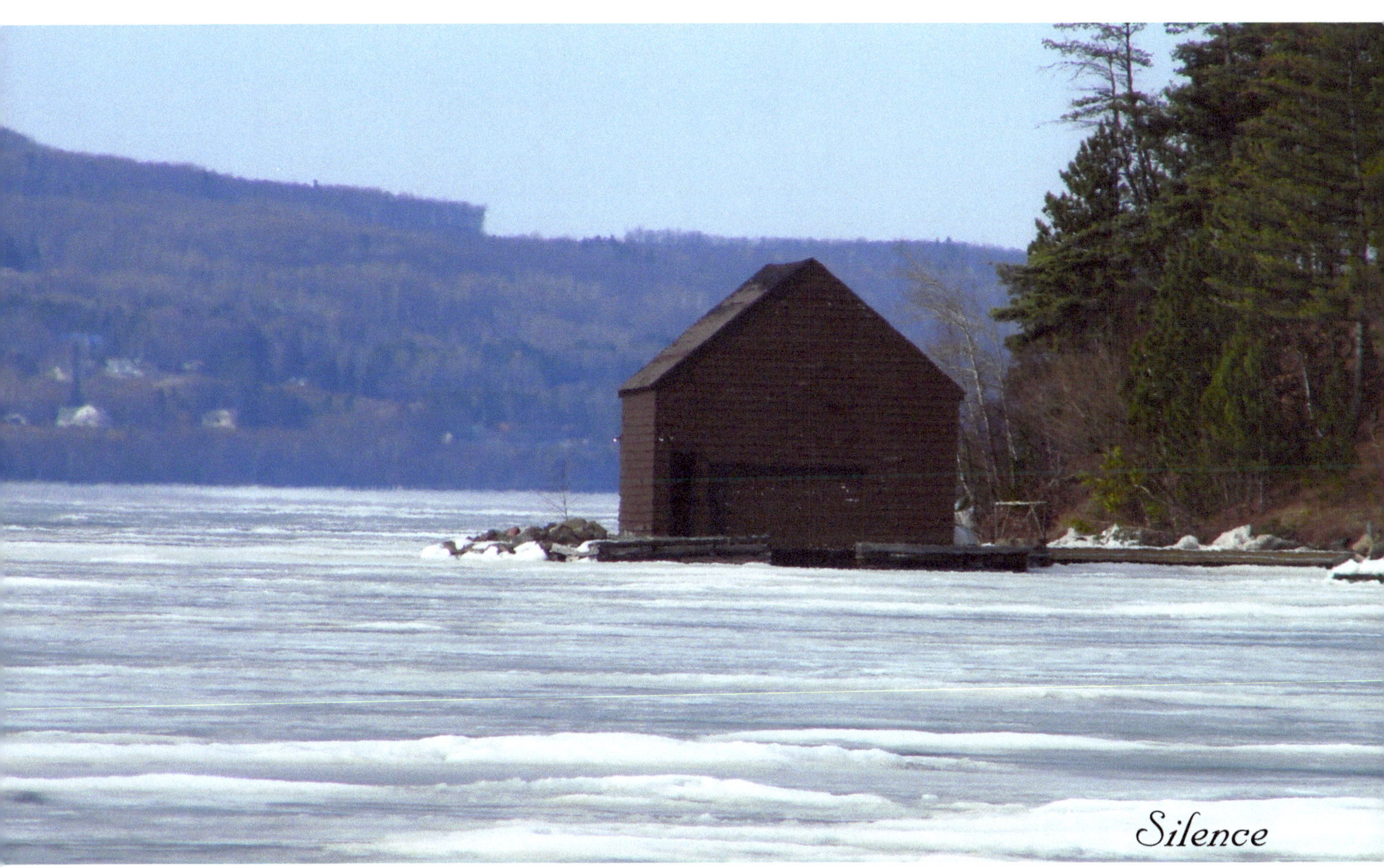

Silence

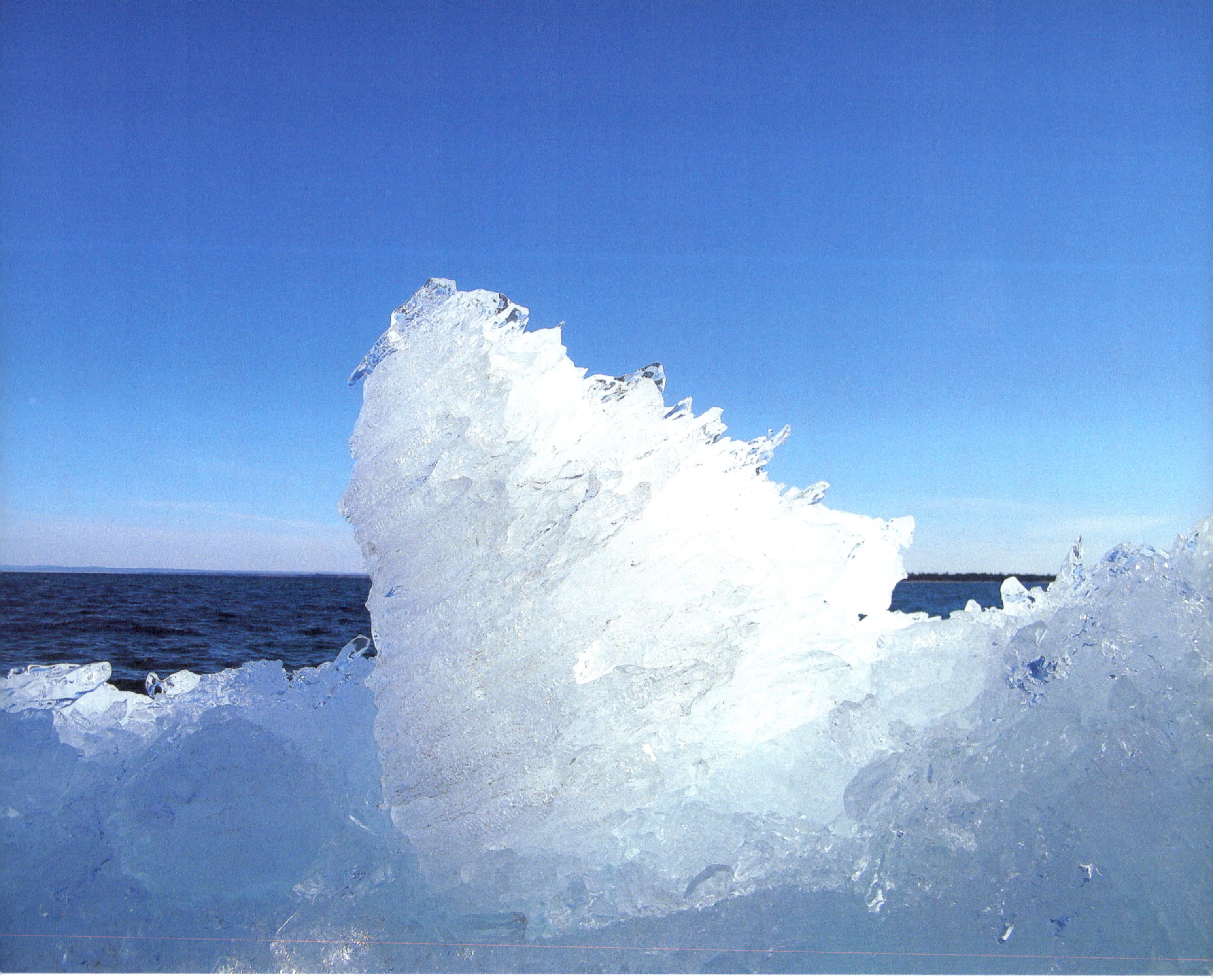

As the ice melts and breaks,

the lake motion pushes the blocks up onto the shore.

This block has been shaped and formed by the wind-blown water.

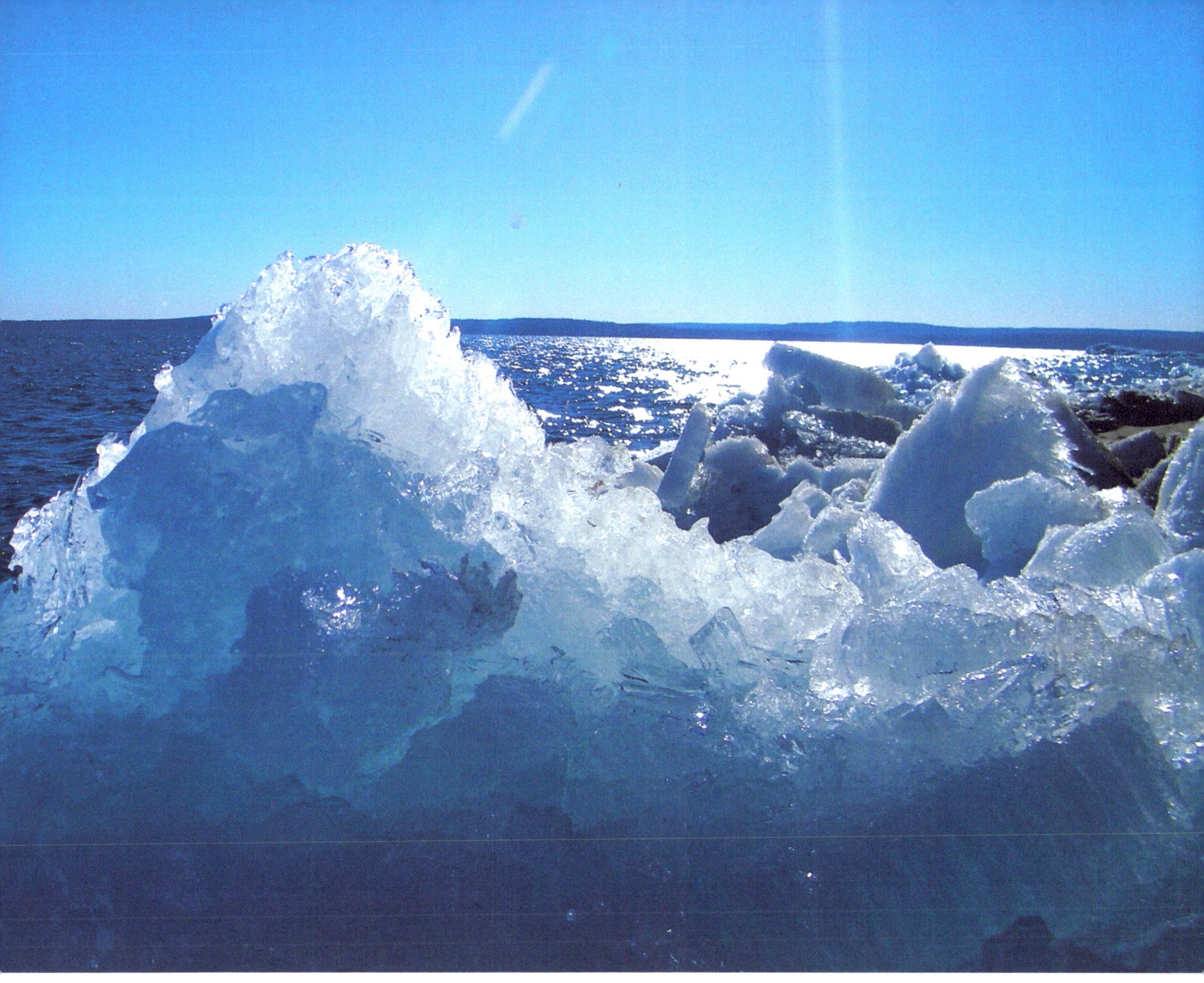

And each block pushes the ones before it

up into the sunshine.

Message from the island for the seasonal residents:

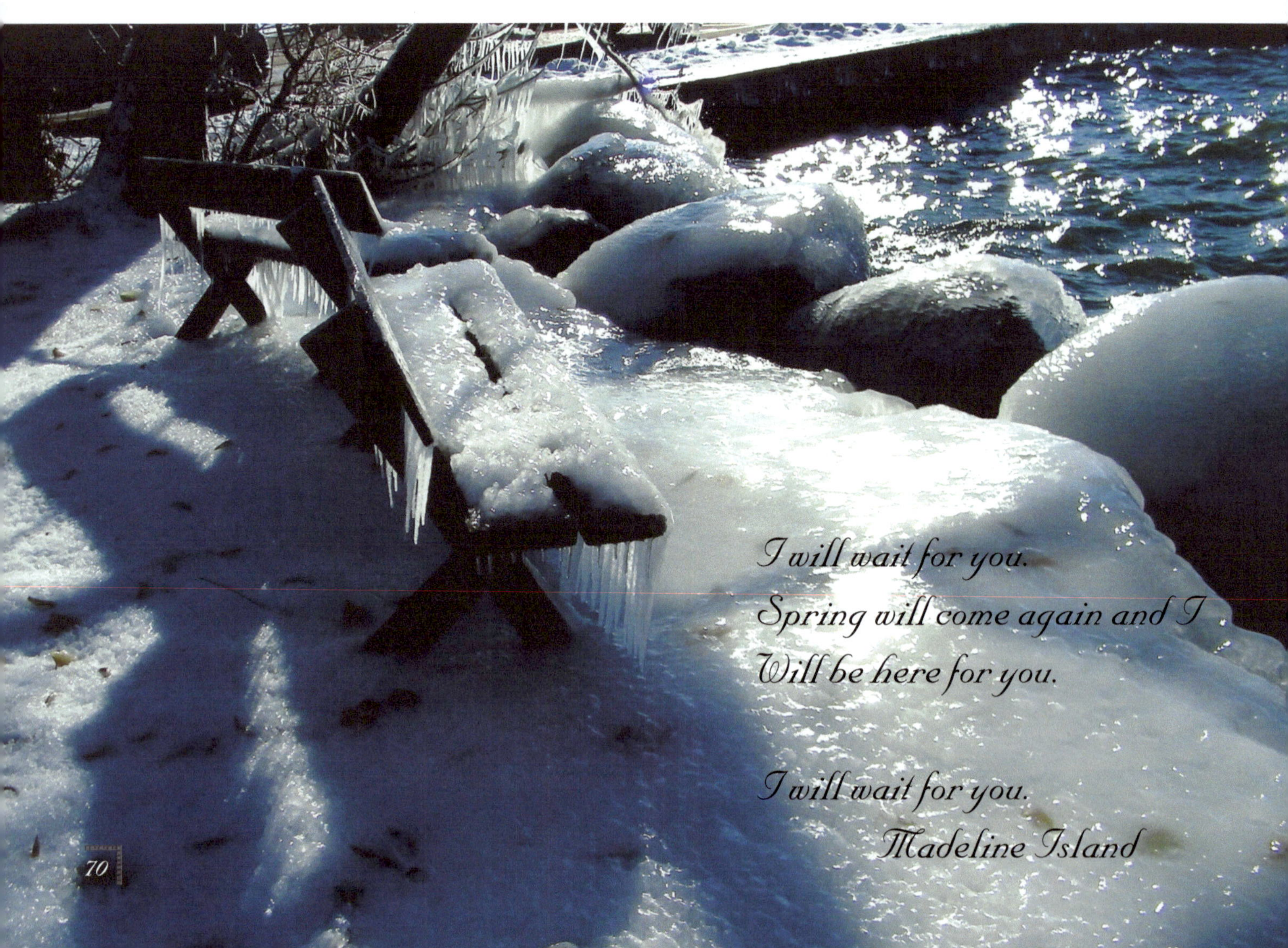

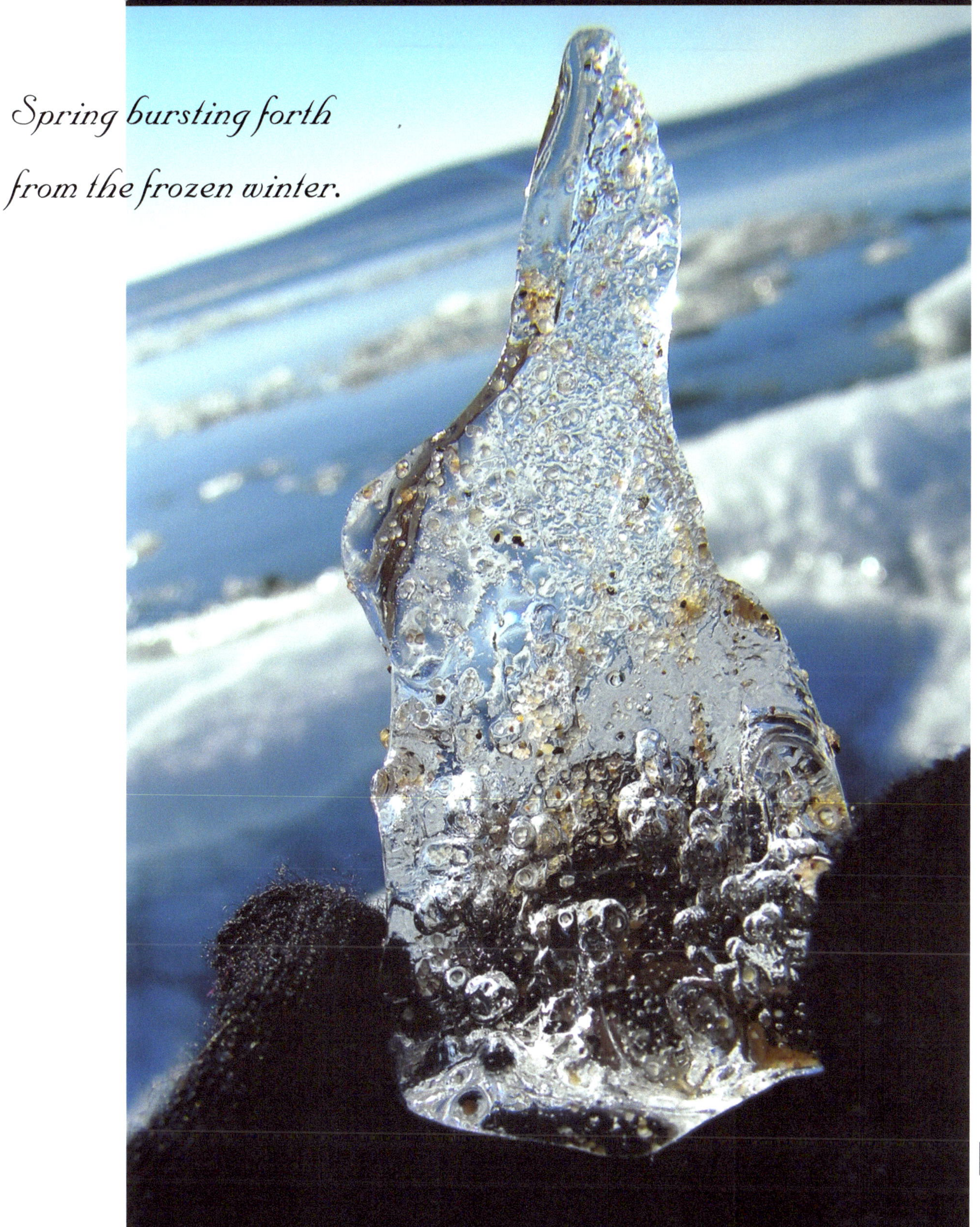

Spring bursting forth

from the frozen winter.

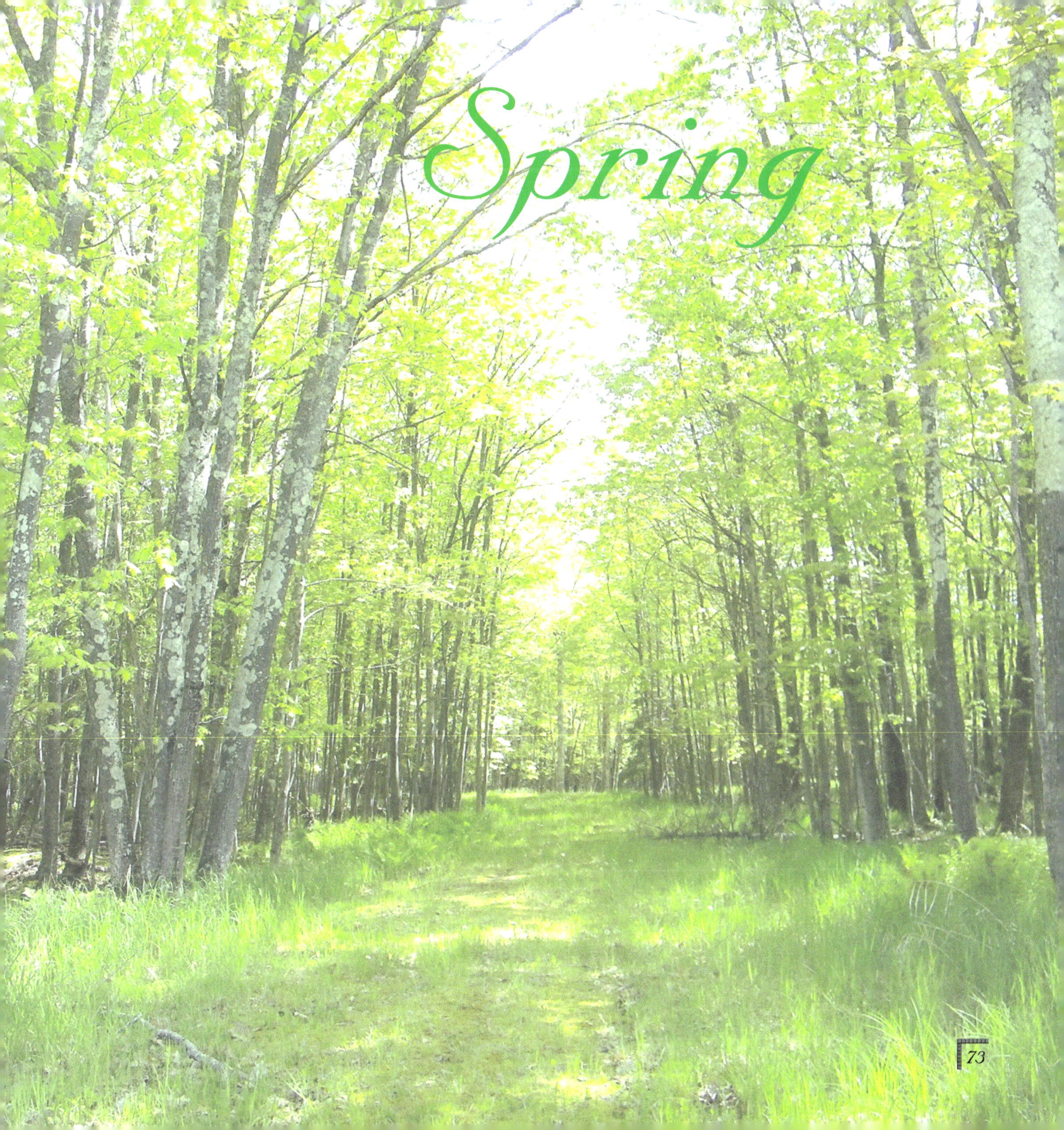
Spring

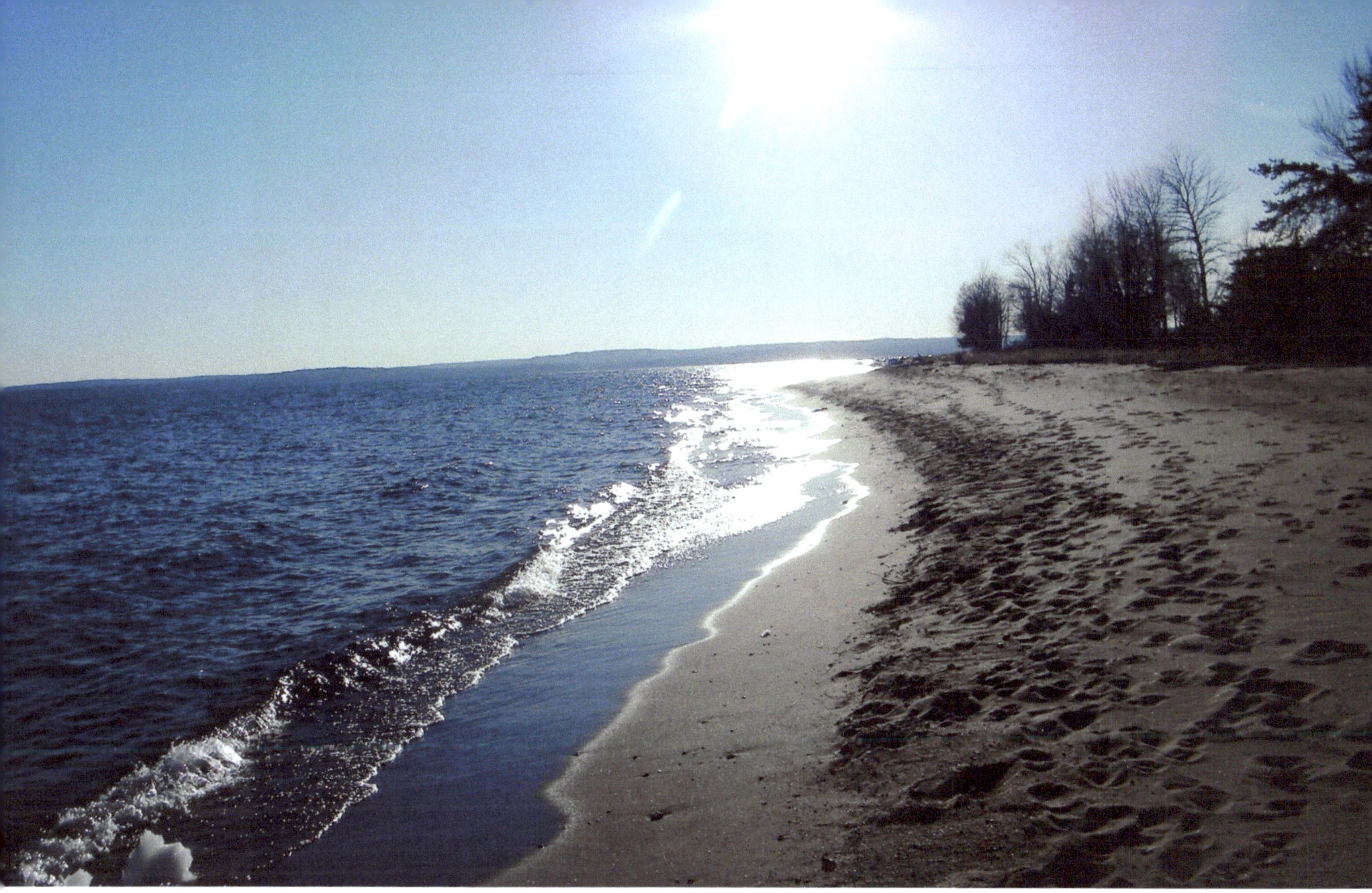

Grant's Point basks in the Spring sunshine.

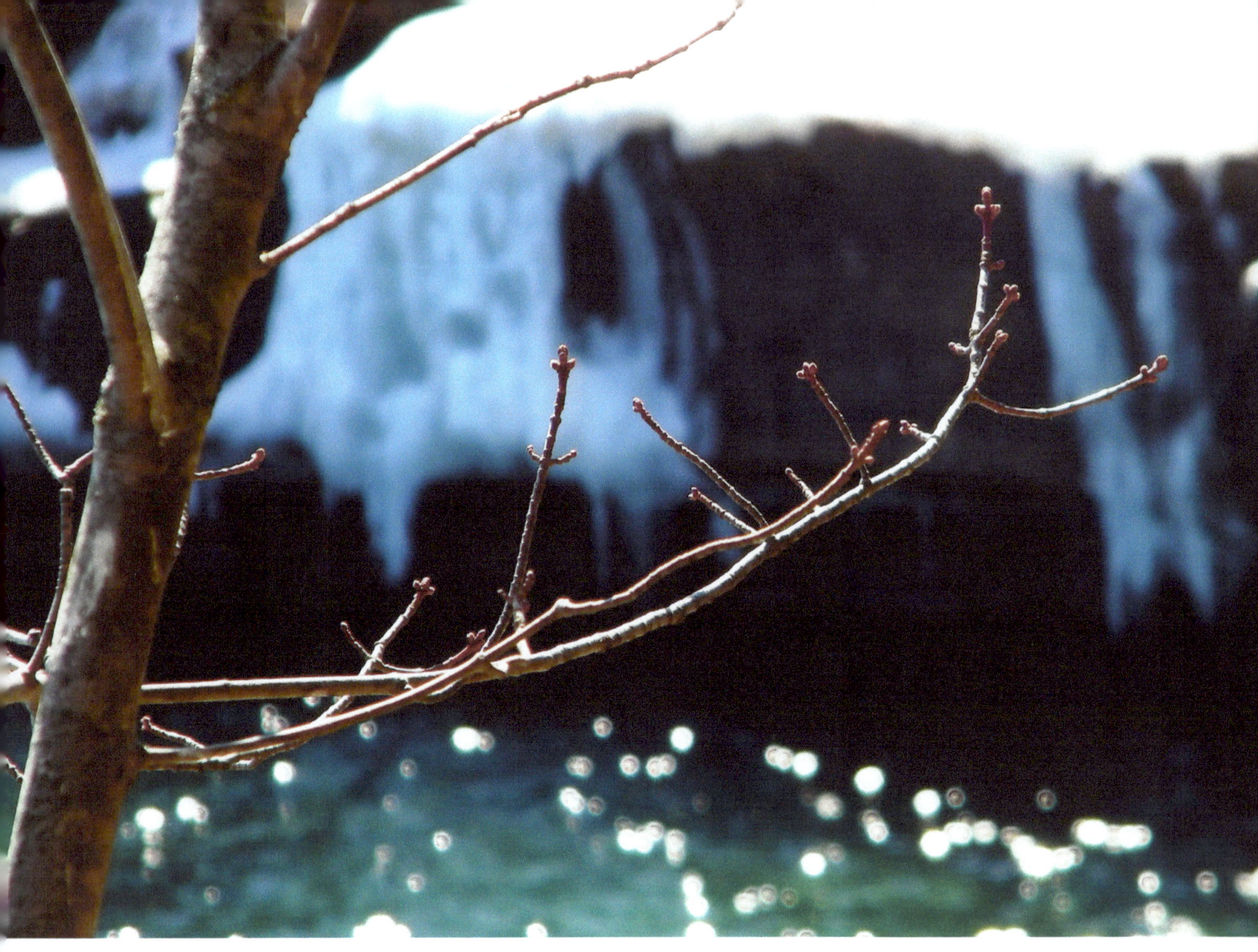

Warm spring sun melts the ice even as it brings forth new growth.

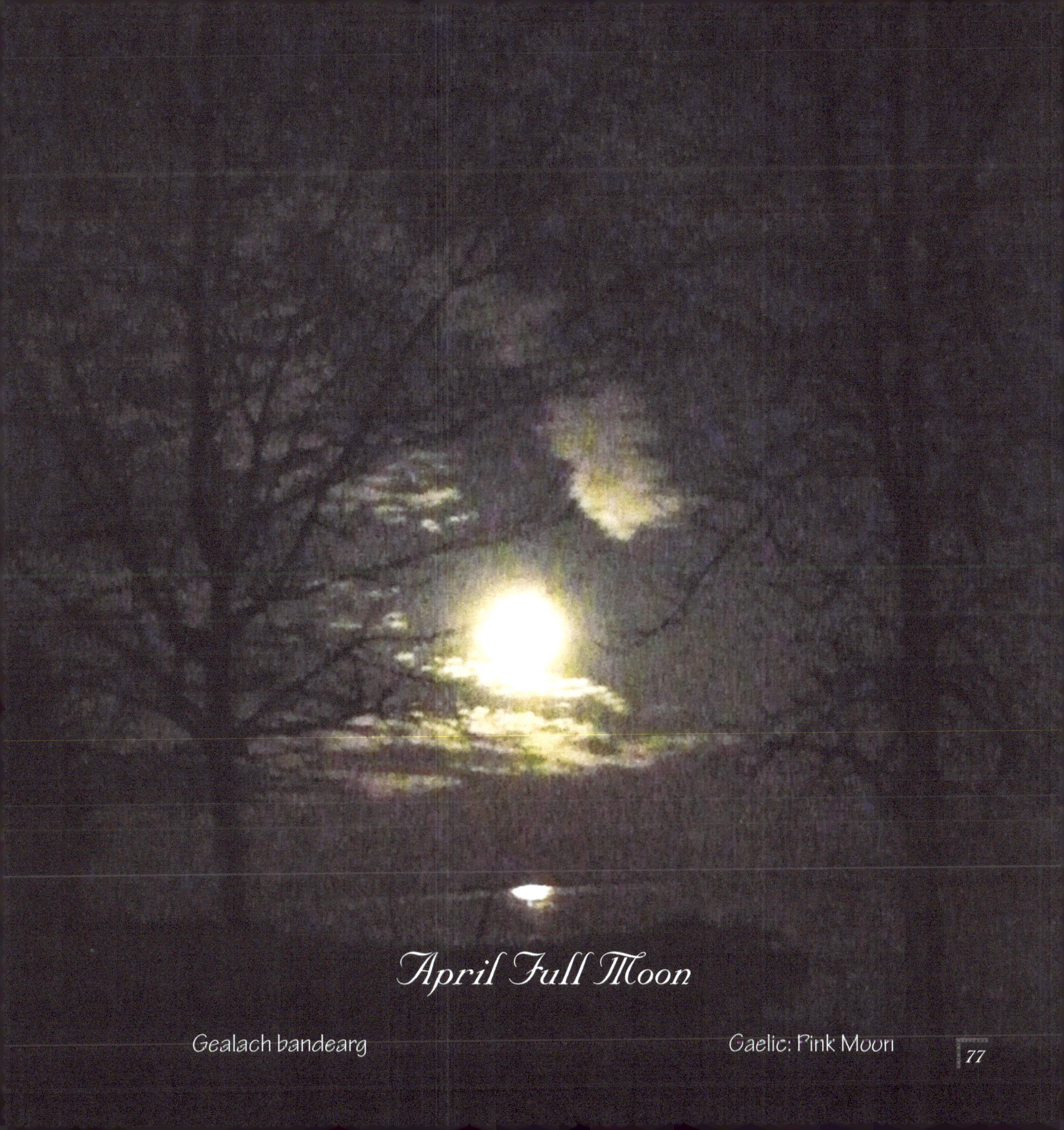

April Full Moon

Gealach bandearg

Gaelic: Pink Moon

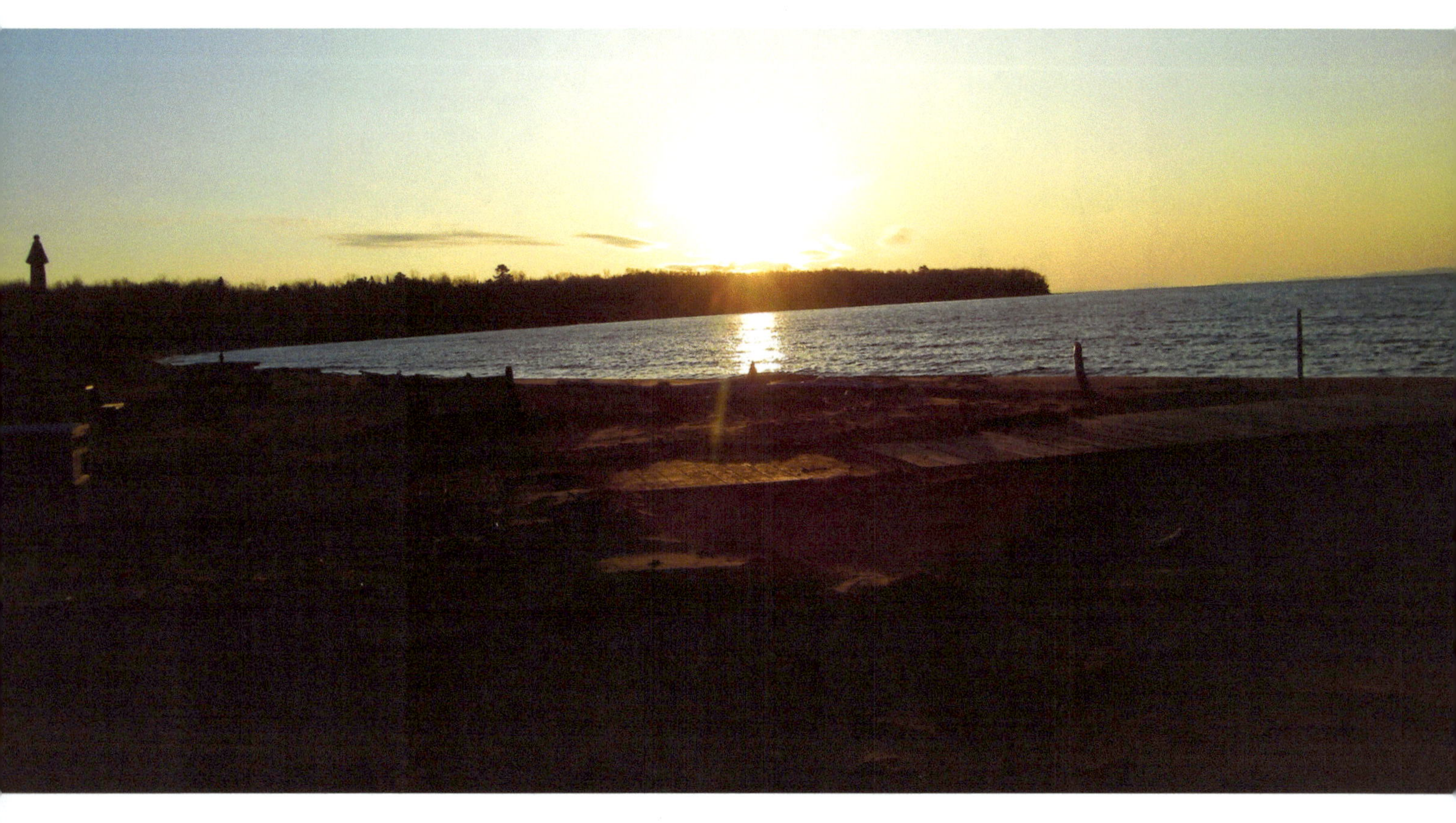

Easter — the Son has risen indeed!

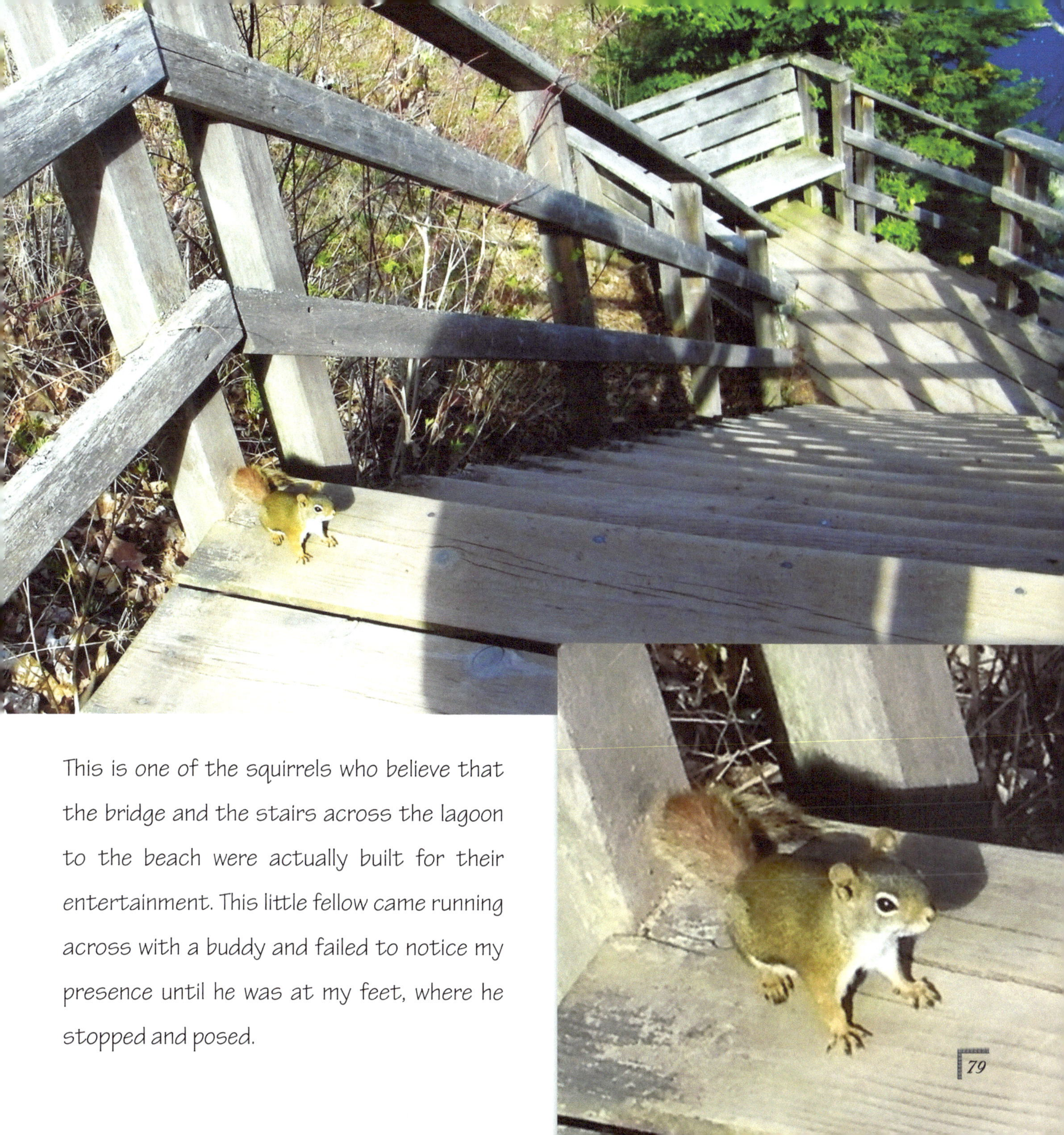

This is one of the squirrels who believe that the bridge and the stairs across the lagoon to the beach were actually built for their entertainment. This little fellow came running across with a buddy and failed to notice my presence until he was at my feet, where he stopped and posed.

No up. No down.

No left. No right.

Just beautiful.

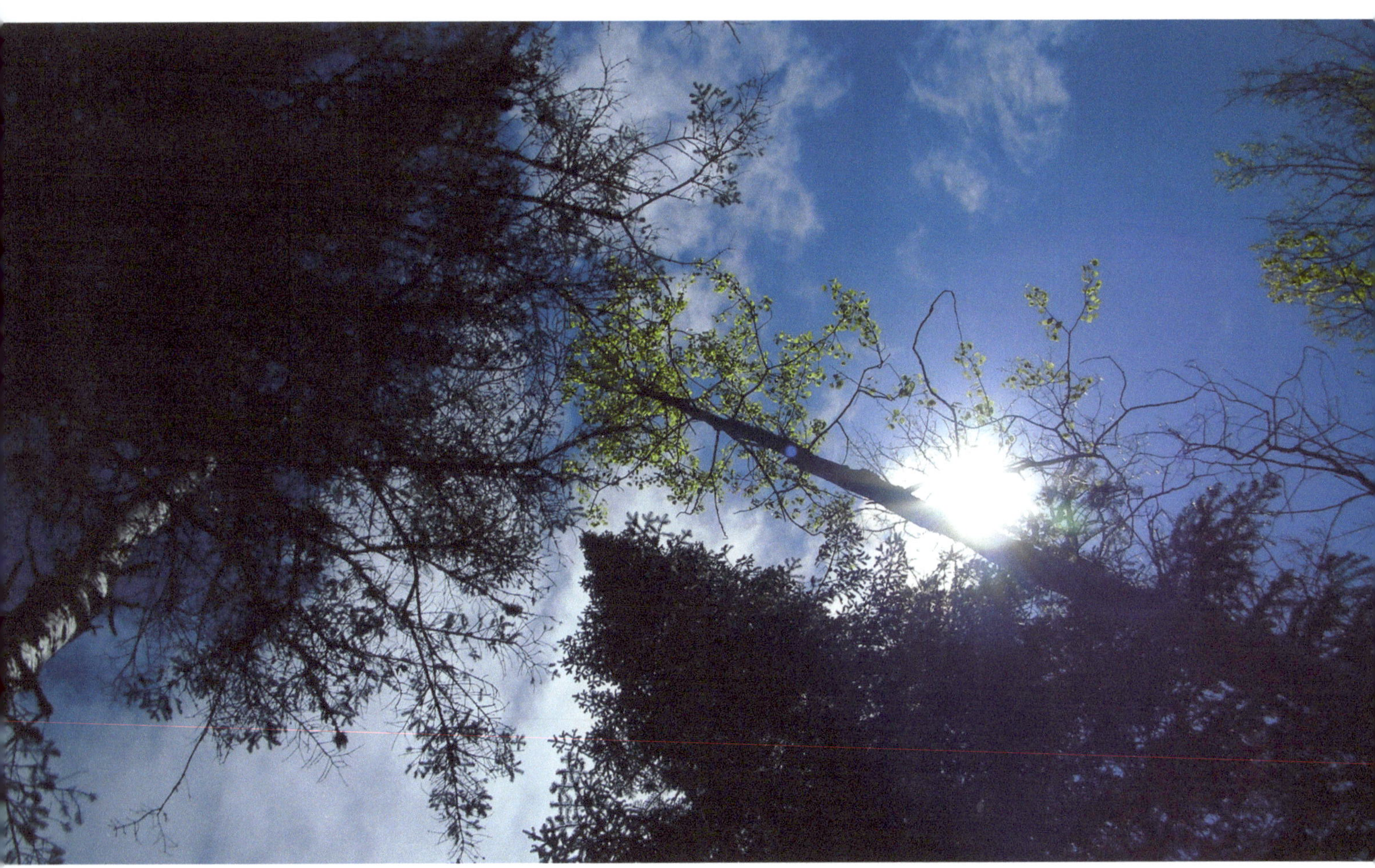

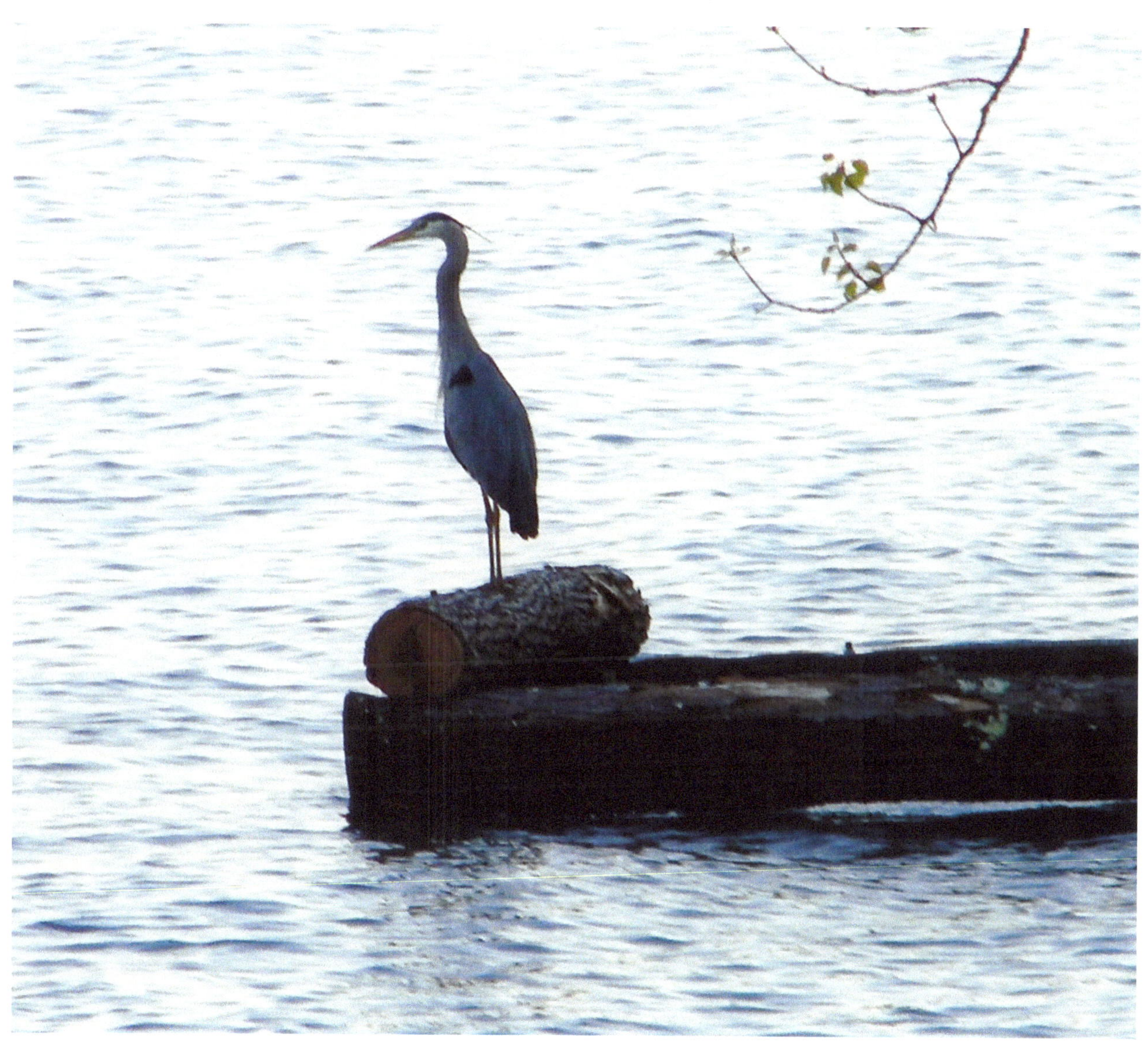

Great Blue Heron - Prince of water and sky.

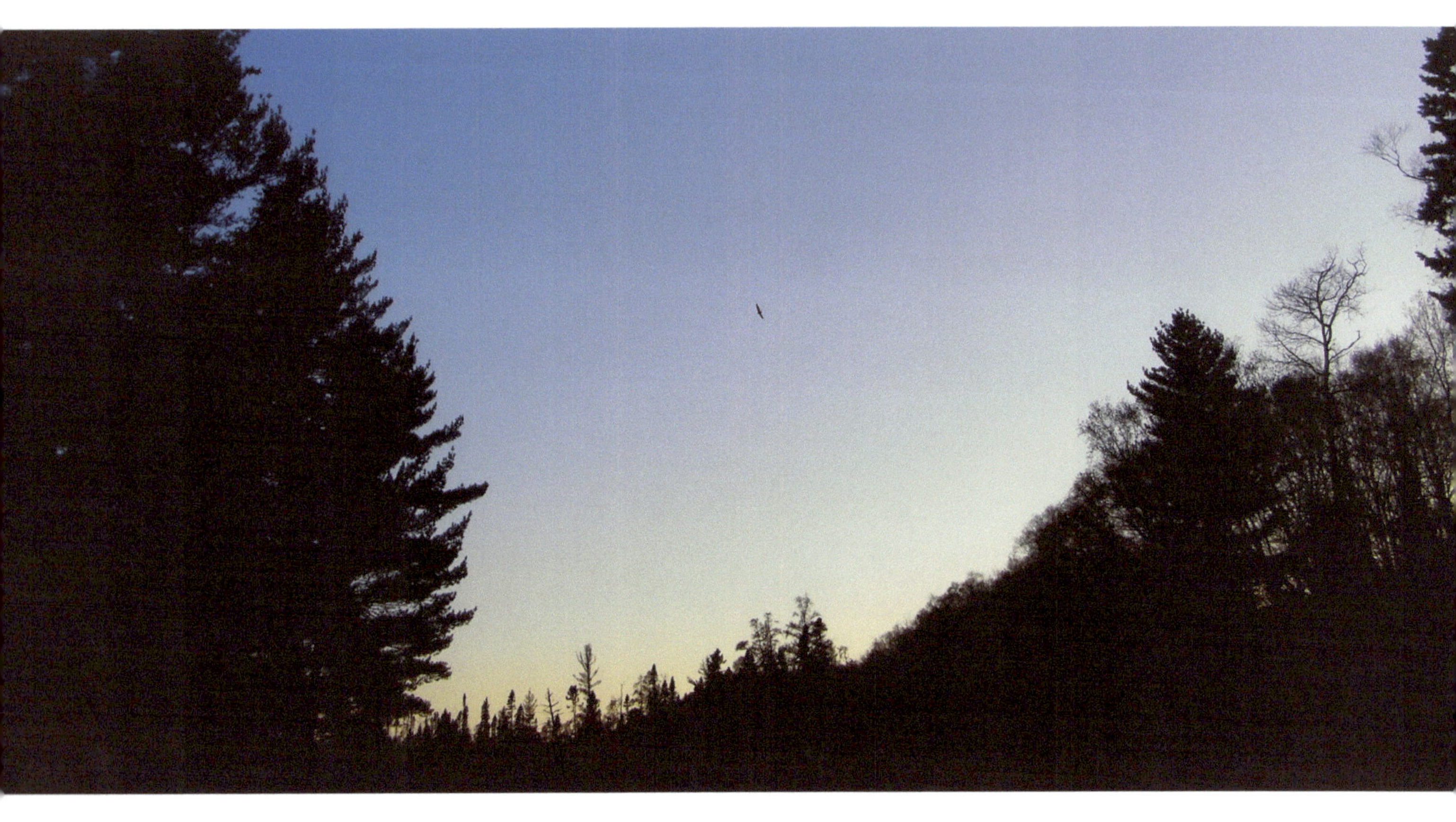

Flying high in the evening sky.

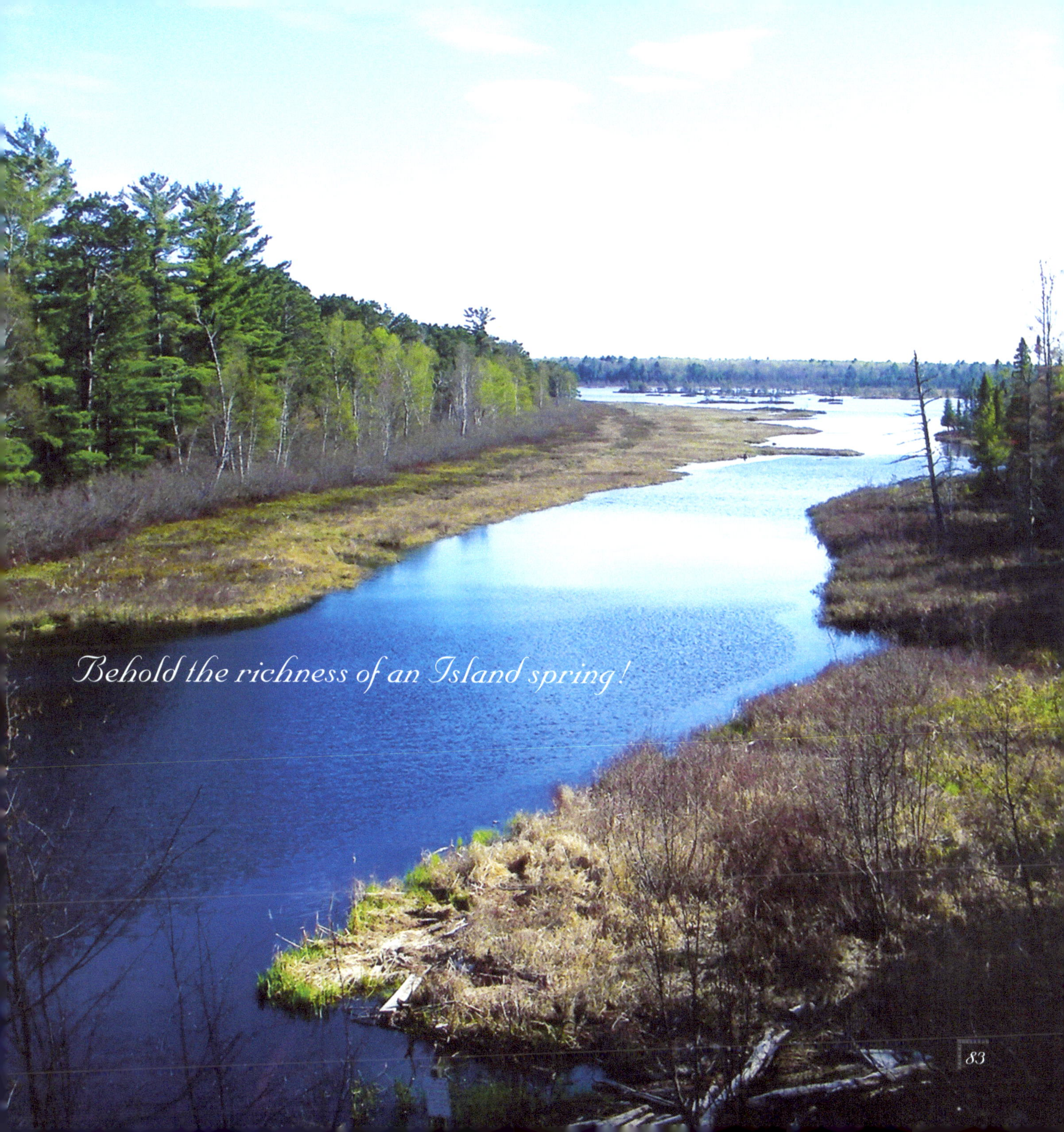
Behold the richness of an Island spring!

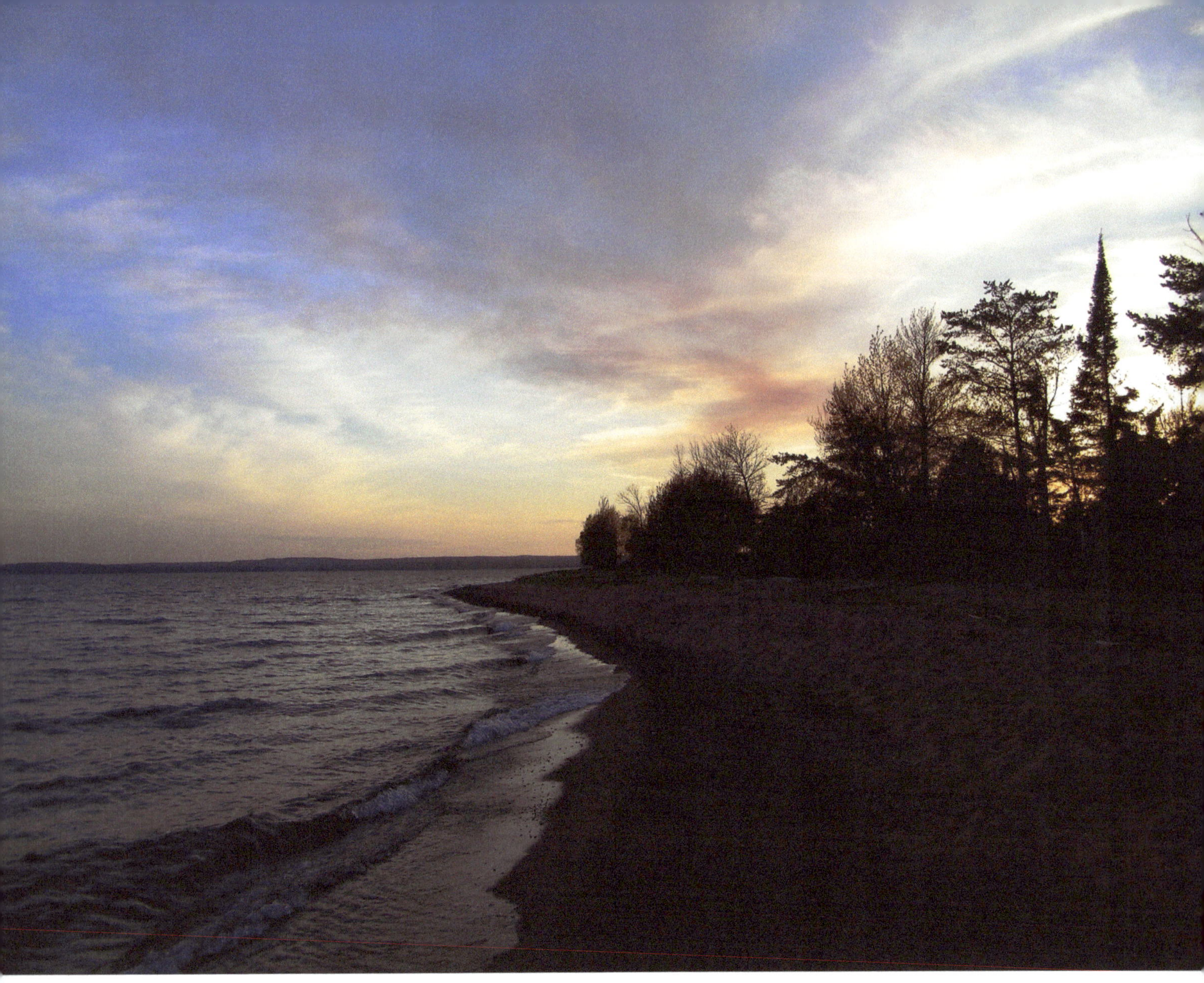

The Island abounds with glorious sunsets in all seasons.

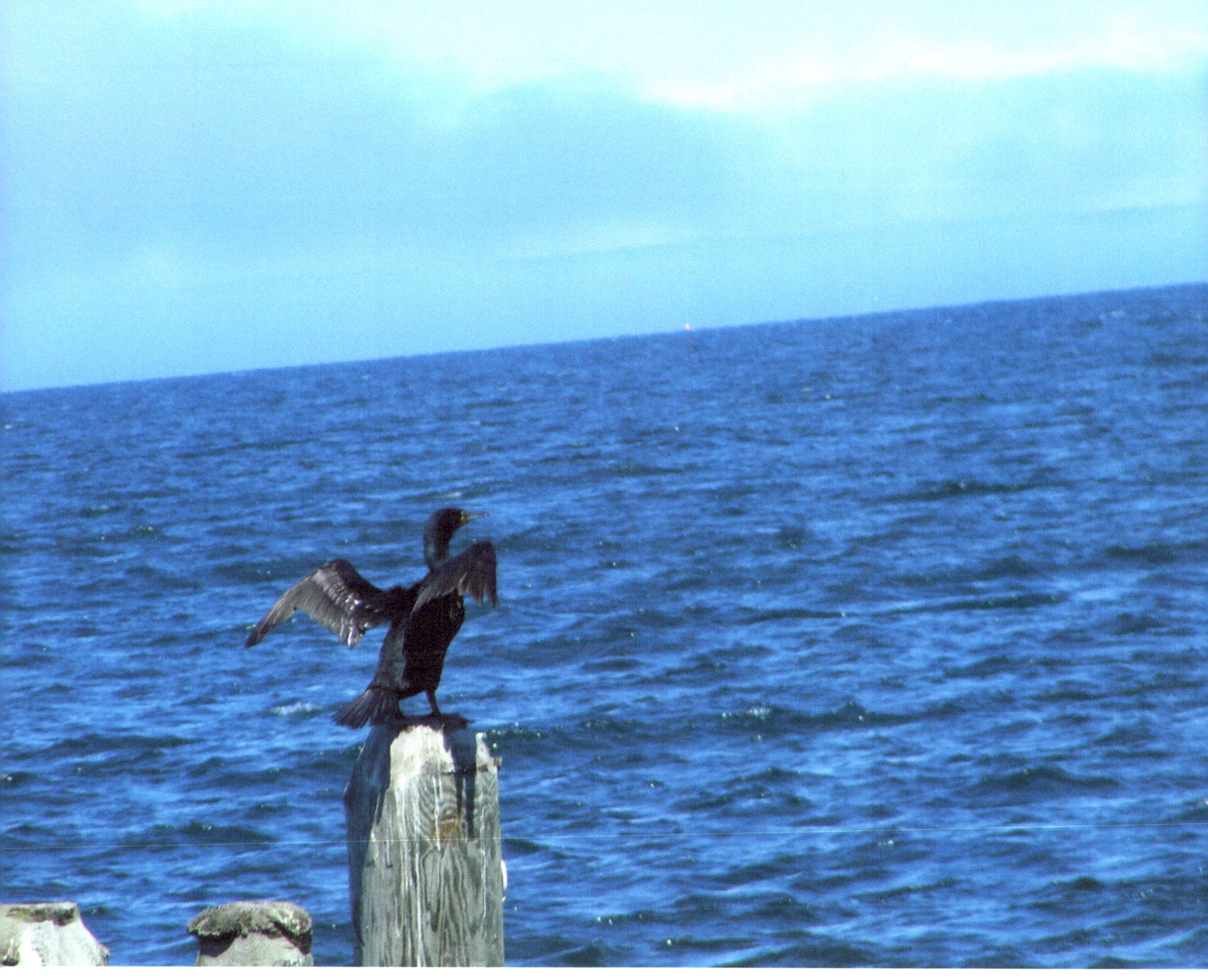

The Cormorant is a bird that can dive to catch his meals.

This means, however, that he has to hang his wings out to dry.

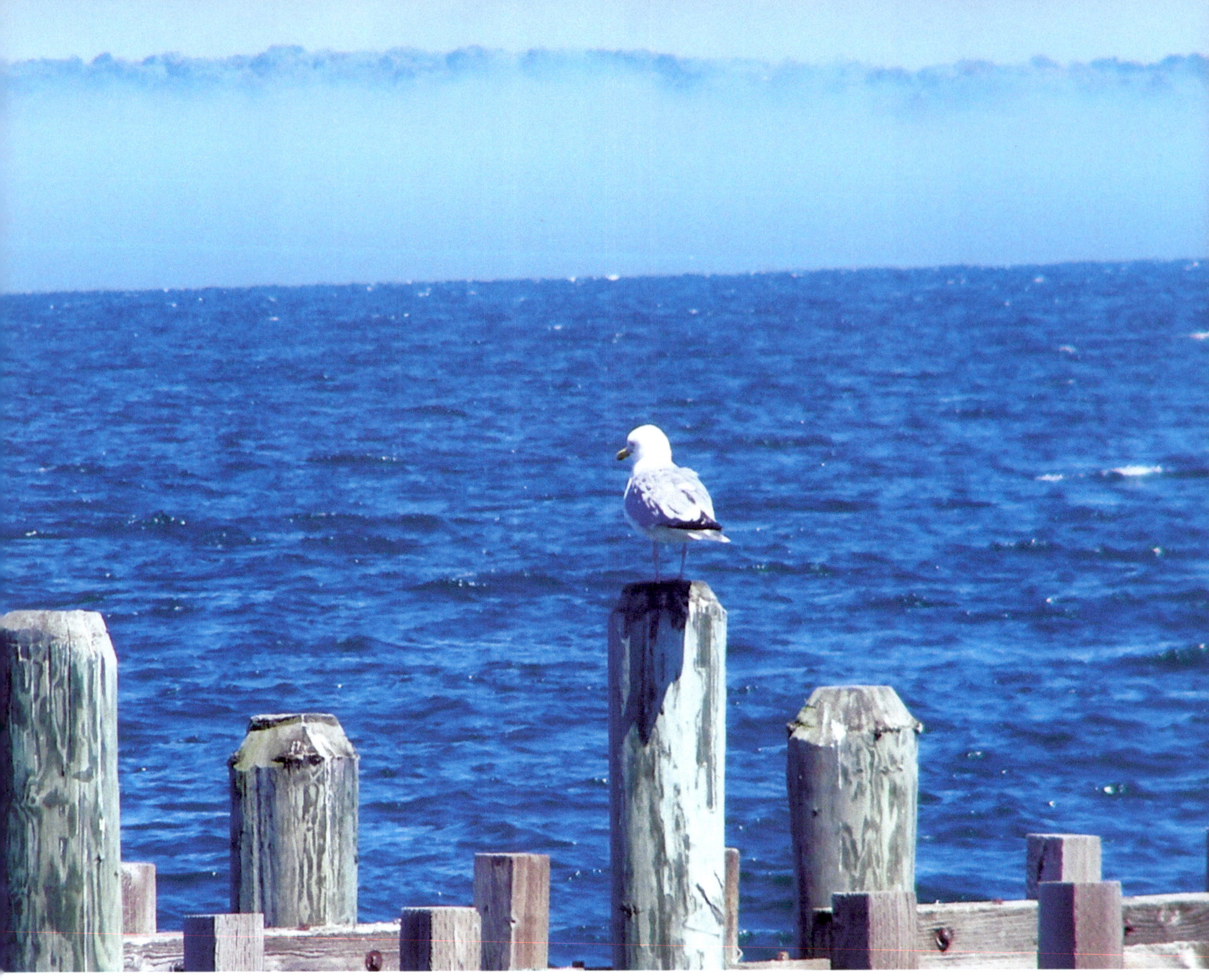

As has been seen, the gulls come in many colors and patterns.

This is one of the prettiest.

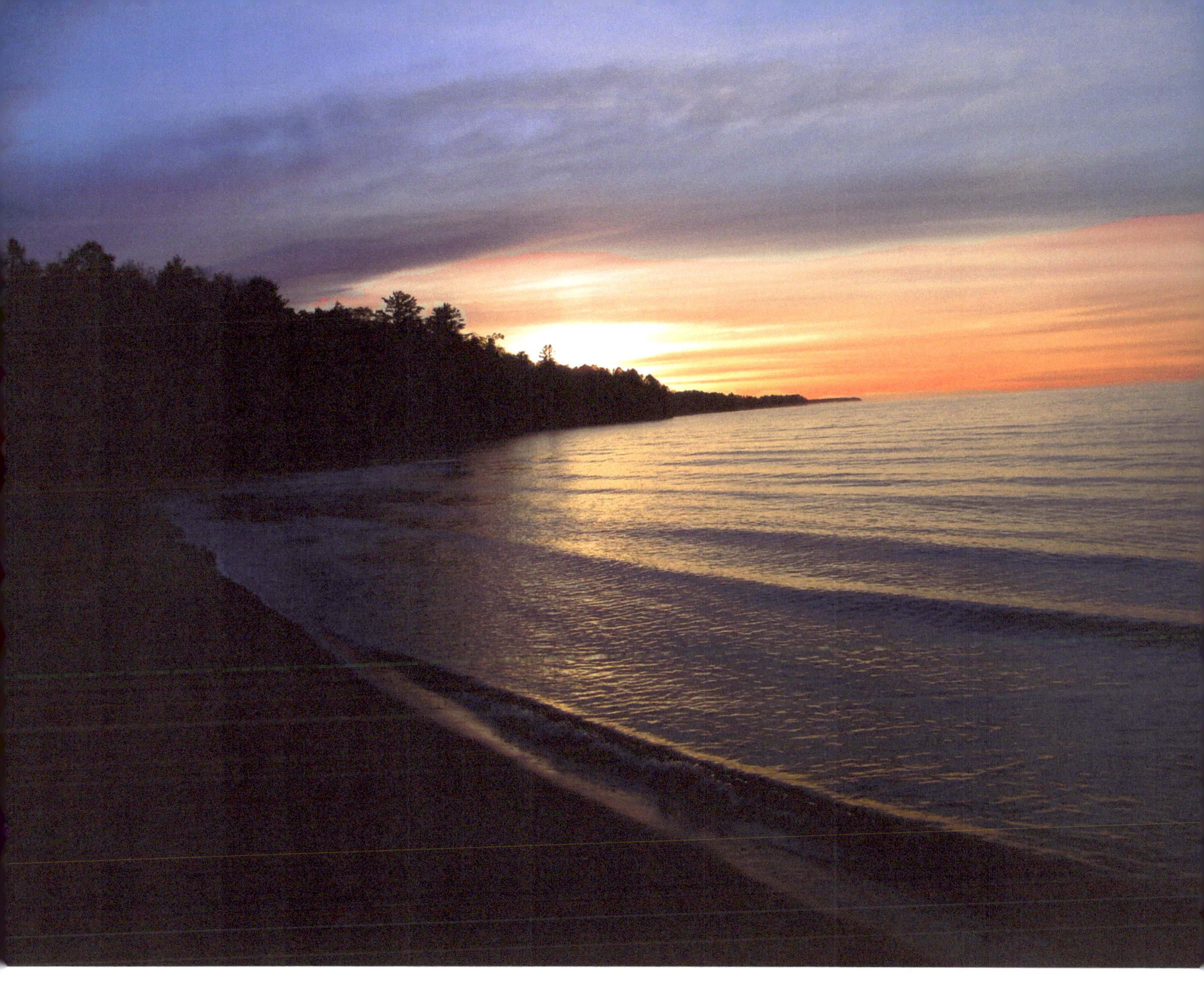

With its new-morning brilliance

the sun makes of land and water and sky

a finer altar than any man could build.

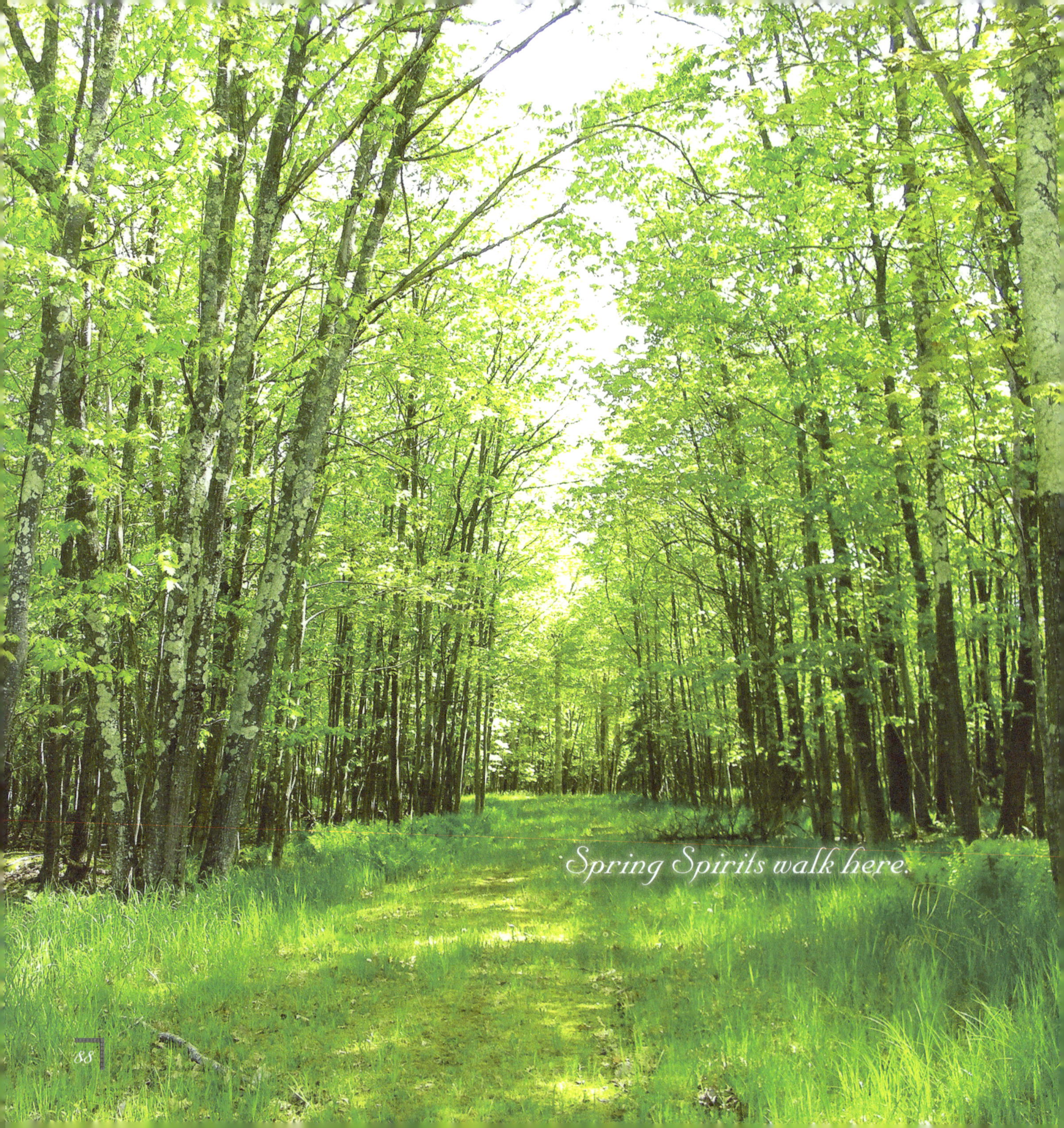
Spring Spirits walk here.

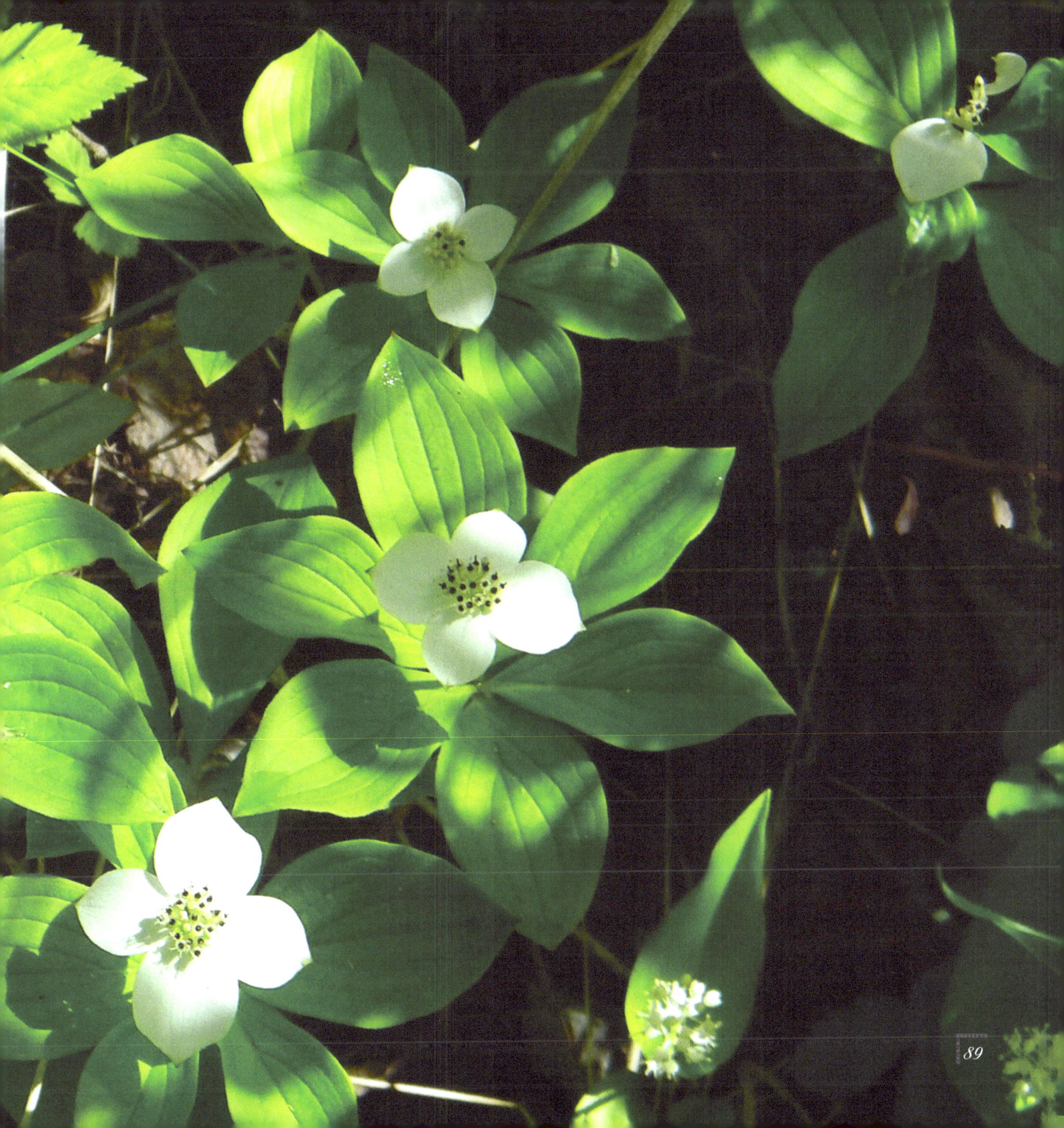

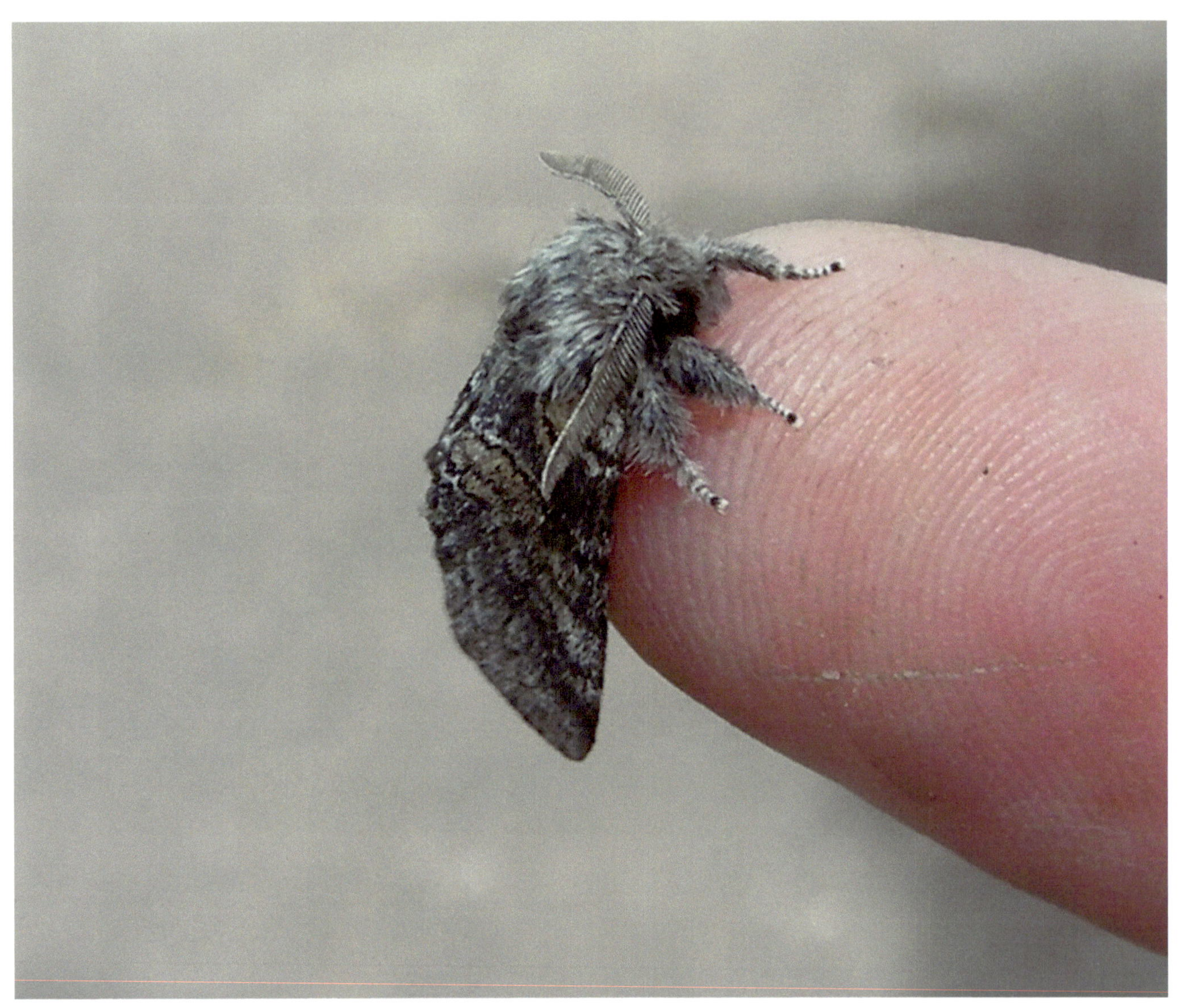

Found this little guy doing the back stroke in the water in my cooler. I scooped him out and set him to dry while I finished packing. When I picked him up on my finger to see if he was ready to fly, he wouldn't leave!

Prints in various sizes, matted, framed, or alone, can be ordered by contacting Motherwell Photography at the contact information below. I'll be happy to send you a price list. Also see the website for additional images of the Land, Lake, and Sky of Madeline Island.

Sheelagh Dalziel
Motherwell Photography
motherwellphoto@gmail.com

www.motherwellphotography.com

Index

Summer

Autumn

Winter

Spring

Sheelagh Dalziel was born and raised in Ohio, atten ded high school in Pennsylvania, started college in Virginia and finish ed college back in her home state. After a short stint in Cleveland, she followed her parents down to Tennessee where she worked for the University of Tennessee and later earned a Masters degree there.

In 1987, Sheelagh moved to Raleigh, NC. After many years and adventures, she moved back to Pennsylvania in 2009. After being unemployed for a year and a half a conversation with her brother on Madeline Island led to his wife inviting Sheelagh to move up to their farm. And so she came across the water to Madeline Island in the Spring of 2014.

Sheelagh has taken pictures all her life but found in that summer an artistry for photography focusing on the spiritual aspects of the Island.

All photographs were taken with a Kodak EasyShare Z1015 IS camera.

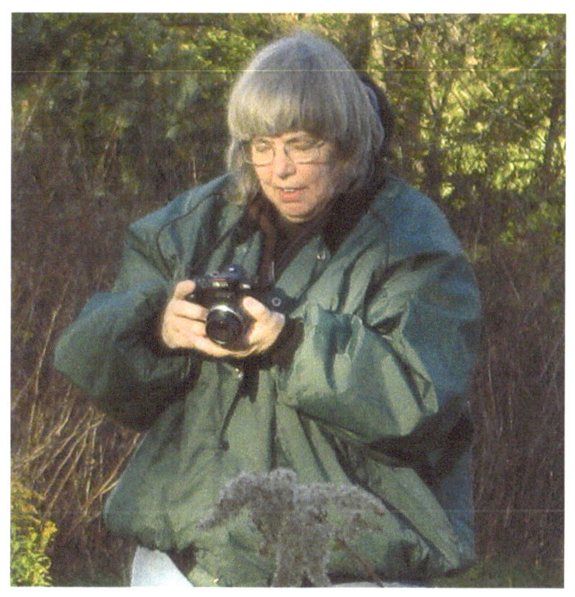